VW Beetle Convertible

Karmann Ghia
Rometsch

1949-1980

D0930979

VW BEETLE CONVERTIBLE
Karmann Ghia - Rometsch
1949-1980

A Documentation by Walter Zeichner

Schiffer Publishing Ltd

West Chester, Pennsylvania 19380

This volume is dedicated to the open VW Beetle. This automobile, a popular variant of the all-time world-champion production car, enjoys a great popularity, and it was obvious that the open Karmann Ghia and several derivatives of the open Beetle á la Denzel, Enzmann, Rometsch and Colani should be considered too. We have tried to portray the vehicles from contemporary brochures and catalogs, just as they appeared in advertisements at the time. VW advertising always was characterized by a significant style—on an international level, and it is precisely the style of the advertising graphics of those times that make it so interesting to look back upon. Thus this little book is not going to offer any directions for repair or restoration; it is meant rather to be a picture book of automobile nostalgia, and is intended to transport the reader back to a time that, while it may not lie too far in the past, is nevertheless history....

We must not forget to thank helpful collaborators who placed material at our disposition, such as the Wilhelm Karmann GmbH, Georg Amtmann, Kai Jacobsen, Hans-J. Klersy, Reinhard Lintelmann and Robert Horender, who set up the display of models on page 84. Duplication of factory publications was made possible by the kind permission of the Volkswagen AG of Wolfsburg.

Halwart Schrader

Copyright © 1989 by Schiffer Publishing, Ltd..
Library of Congress Catalog Number: 88-63997.

Translated from German by Dr. Edward Force.
Printed in the United States of America.
ISBN: 0-88740-168-6
Published by Schiffer Publishing, Ltd.
1469 Morstein Road, West Chester, Pennsylvania 19380

Originally published under the title "VW Käfer Cabrio" 1949-80, Schrader Motor Chronik, copyright Schrader Automobil-Bücher, Handels-GmbH, München, West Germany, © 1986, ISBN: 3-992617-15-8.

This book may be purchased from the publisher.
Please include $2.00 postage.
Try your bookstore first.

Contents

The VW Convertible—a Classic

On June 3, 1949, the series production of the most-successful convertible of all time began in Osnabrück. The Karmann firm, located there, built a total of 331,847 of the Type 15 Volkswagen convertible from that day until January 10, 1980. A prototype of this model had been introduced in 1947; it was bodied in Wolfsburg but never was put into series production. At that time the Type 15 was a two-seater whose cloth top could be fully lowered. Striking characteristics were the small side windows that tapered sharply backward and the two rows of louvers atop the long rear engine hood.

As of June 1948 there also was a very-little-known four-door Volkswagen convertible which was finished by hand at the Hebmüller firm in Wülfrath, near Wuppertal, for use as a police emergency vehicle. This model, known as Type 18A, existed in two styles. In very small numbers this version was made with four steel doors, while the majority of the total of 482 police convertibles that were built had only canvas doors. The doors could be rolled to the side, and naturally had no windows, so it was very uncomfortable for the police, especially in winter. By the end of 1949, the motor pool was changed to closed types. At this time several four-door convertibles, very similar to the Hebmüller cars, were built by the coachwork firm of Franz Papler in Cologne. A few of these police convertibles of the early postwar era have survived to this day and receive loving care in the hands of collectors.

Simultaneous with the appearance of the four-seat Karmann convertible, a two-seat variant with fully lowering top was offered for sale. It was designed by Hebmüller and called Type 14 at the factory. The prototypes were finished in 1948. These cars were put to exhaustive tests in Wolfsburg before the green light was given for production in Wülfrath.

Hebmüller received the order to build 2000 of the elegant two-seaters. VW expected this model to sell well, as it featured the best of series production, even though the price of 7500 Marks was considerably higher than the 5300-Mark price of the standard sedan. But suddenly all their dreams were shattered when, one month after productionbegan, a devastating fire destroyed almost all of the Hebmüller firm's production facilities. With utmost effort and great financial support, their production was set in motion again relatively quickly, but the production capacity was reduced sharply. The firm's economic position worsened to the point where work proceeded slowly. In May of 1952 Hebmüller proposed a compromise. Only 696 of the open Volkswagen had been built by the summer of that year. A remainder of perhaps a dozen two-seaters then was produced at Karmann, and then it was all over with the sporting convertible.

The four-seat version that Karmann had produced since 1949 on the basis of the VW export model originally cost 7500 Marks, as did the Hebmüller car. This price was 1875 Marks more than the export version of the sedan, which was equipped with additional chrome trim and a more luxurious interior. At first only one or two cars a day were finished in Osnabrück, where they sold immediately. From the start the VW convertible had its group of devoted fans. It was scarcely possible at that time to get a more reasonably priced convertible of that size with four full-size seats.

Whoever had the good fortune to be able to afford a real convertible in 1950 had the following choices in Germany: DKW Meisterklasse, Ford Taunus (rebodied by Deutsch in Cologne), Borgward Hansa 1500 (at the high price of 10,500 Marks), and the Mercedes-Benz 170 convertible (for 12,500 Marks).

The open Beetle was therefore a thoroughly tempting offer. The Volkswagen enjoyed an excellent reputation from the start. It was economical and undemanding, and ran at a genuine 62 mph. Making a choice in that market was not a very difficult one for many convertible customers.

Happily, the price of the open Volkswagen sank in the years before 1961. Despite the many improvements that were added to it, the price reached only 5990 Marks. To be sure, the price went up again after that and reached 14,423 Marks by the end of production in January of 1980.

The last VW convertibles built in Osnabrück scarcely had a single component in common with the models from the beginning era, even though the cars resembled one another strongly from the outside. Features that were improved steadily included the arrangement of the Beetle's lights, the view all around (windshields and rear windows), and the interior decor. Only one thing had been kept the same: the running boards. They were a fixed component of even the last Beetle convertibles of 1980, as well as of all subsequent sedans made in Mexico, Nigeria and Brazil.

Prototype of the convertible by Hebmüller. Note the elegantly shaped louvers on the rear hood.

In 1957 the Beetle convertible was joined by a sporty, elegant version with a flat coupe body designed by the Italian firm of Ghia, and likewise produced by Karmann. The driving force behind the production of this car was once again Wilhelm Karmann, who had had the idea in the early fifties of producing a pretty coupe on the proven Volkswagen chassis. Such a prototype was built by Ghia of Turin in 1955. When it was shown that summer, the public accepted it enthusiastically, and the press described it as one of the most beautiful vehicles of the time.

After a few small revisions to the body, series production of the Karmann Ghia coupe began in August of 1955. The new car, which also was also offered in the official VW sales program, found buyers quickly. The Karmann Ghia particularly was popular among the ladies, since they usually gave less importance to fast performance than to a chic exterior, so that the 30 horsepower that the VW engine offered gave this "sports car" enough power. Naturally, the Karmann Ghia was ridiculed by many for this reason as the "I wish I had a Porsche" car, but that had little effect on the car's popularity.

At the Frankfurt Auto Show in September of 1957, the Karmann Ghia convertible was displayed. Fortunately, nobody thought about roll bars at that time, and so the car showed good breeding and elegance with its hood up. As far as the finish of the car and the choice of harmonious seat patterns were concerned, an astounding variety were offered. There even were metallic colors, and the top could, if desired, be set off in a different suitable color. Such a convertible was not exactly cheap at 8250 Marks, but there was scarcely a two-seater convertible (disregarding the emergency seats) that not only offered such quality and comfort but also was such fun to drive at such a reasonable price. In Germany there were few people who wanted to go adventuring with a Fiat 1200 Spyder or an Austin-Healey Sprite, and other pretty cars like the Renault Floride or the Simca Océane scarcely were known there. But everybody knew the advantages and the outstanding workmanship of the Wolfsburg products, even if this one wore an Italian dress.

In the course of its production run, the obligatory improvements to the Karmann Ghia naturally took place. In 1960 the power was increased by four horsepower, and it could now be ordered with a new fully synchronized four-speed gearbox. In the summer of 1965 the pretty car received an improved front axle and a 1300 cc motor with 40 horsepower, followed in the very next year by a 44-horsepower engine of 1.5-liter displacement. At the same time the car gained front disc brakes and a dual braking system. In the summer of 1970 performance reached its absolute high point of 50 horsepower from 1584 cc, and the car easily reached 87 mph. Still, this was not very high for a sports car, but one could no longer say the car was underpowered.

The power remained at this level until the close of 1973, when the end came for the Karmann Ghia Type 14 after eighteen years of production.

By 1973, 445,300 cars, 80,899 of them convertibles, had been sold, confirming the Wolfsburg auto firm's hold on the market with this elegant Volkswagen. Demand had decreased in the last production years on account of the body styling, which by then had become old-fashioned.

Today the Type 14 and the convertible in particular rank among the desirable collector cars, though the prices of good examples still generally remain within reasonable limits.

VOLKSWAGEN *Cabriolet*

2 Sitzer

A Choice of Two Models

When the basic concept of the Volkswagen originated at the end of the thirties, the convertible had been ruled out in favor of a convertible sedan. Then came the war, and only a few closed Beetles were produced for Nazi officials and their representatives. When actual Volkswagen production began after the war, a convertible version was considered again. In the end two coachbuilding firms were given contracts to build convertibles on the basis of the Beetle: Karmann of Osnabrück and Hebmüller of Wülfrath near Wuppertal.

Ein Gedicht !

Formschön
Elegant
Faszinierend
Temperamentvoll

Mit Recht hat das Cabriolet viele Freunde.

denn es bietet ihnen zu jeder Zeit das Schönste:
Freude an Sonne und Bergen,
angenehme Geborgenheit bei Wind und Wetter.

1949

A rare document from 1949: sales brochure for the two-seat convertible built by the Hebmüller firm in Wülfrath. About 700 cars of this type were built until 1952.

A Poem!

Beautiful in form
Elegant
Fascinating
Full of temperament

The Convertible deserves to have many friends

for it offers them the nicest things every time: Happiness in the sun and the mountains, pleasant protection from wind and weather.

Zwei sehr bequeme Sitze —
Während der Fahrt verstellbar
Zwei Notsitze im Wageninneren
Reichlich bemessener Gepäckraum

Versenkbares Verdeck
Modernes Zweispeichen-Lenkrad
Stilvoll ausgestattetes Armaturenbrett
Geschmackvolle Farbzusammenstellungen

Two very comfortable seats—
Adjustable during the trip
Two more seats if needed
Abundant luggage space

Lowering top
Modern two-spoke steering wheel
Stylishly designed dashboard
Tasteful color combinations

Perhaps an even rarer
brochure from
Switzerland, where in
addition to the sedan
and convertible a
convertible sedan, never
officially offered
otherwise, was
advertised. It was not
produced.

Now three VW models

SEDAN 6250 Francs
4-5 seater—6 hp—includes heater and defroster

During the last eight years the VW has proved itself thirty-six-thousandfold in Russian winters, the hot sandstorms of Africa and the inhospitable areas of the Far North. No vehicle ever has been put to such a long and hard test before it came onto the market. Never yet has a car in the lower-price class combined so many revolutionary improvements—and never before have motorists in all lands said such a spontaneous and unqualified YES to a car!

Since the signing of the new trade treaty with Germany, the VW leads all cars imported into Switzerland. Never before has a car conquered the market in such a short time.

CONVERTIBLE SEDAN 6900 Francs
4/5-seater—6 hp—including heater and defroster

CONVERTIBLE
2/4-seater—6 hp—available soon

The VW is the most popular car in Switzerland today:
—extraordinarily good roadholding (low center of gravity, torsion-bar suspension)
—nimble and fast in the mountains (16.5-foot turning circle)
—low fuel consumption (approx. 7.5 quarts/62 miles)
—high traveling speed (approx. 68 mph)
—modern form (wind tunnel-tested)
—good view (6 windows, short front hood)
—air-cooled motor (no boiling in summer, no frost damage in winter)

Jetzt drei VW Modelle

LIMOUSINE FR. 6250.-
4/5-Plätzer . 6 PS . inkl. Heizung und Defroster

Der VW hat sich während den letzten acht Jahren im russischen Winter, den heißen Sandstürmen Afrikas und in den unwirtlichen Gebieten des hohen Nordens 36 000-fach bewährt. Kein Fahrzeug ist je einer so langen und harten Prüfung unterzogen worden, bevor es auf den Markt kam. Noch nie hat ein Wagen der niedrigen Preisklasse so viele revolutionäre Verbesserungen in sich vereinigt — und nie zuvor hat der Automobilismus in allen Ländern zu einem Wagen so spontan und vorbehaltlos JA gesagt!
Seit Abschluß des neuen Handelsvertrages mit Deutschland steht der VW an der Spitze aller in die Schweiz eingeführten Automobile. Nie zuvor hat sich ein Wagen in so kurzer Zeit den Markt erobert.

CABRIO-LIMOUSINE FR. 6900.-
4/5-Plätzer . 6 PS . inklusive Heizung und Defroster

CABRIOLET
2/4-Plätzer . 6 PS . demnächst lieferbar

**Der VW ist heute
der populärste Wagen der Schweiz:**

— außergewöhnlich gute Straßenhaltung
  (tiefe Schwerpunktlage, Torsionsstab-Federung)
— wendig und schnell am Berg
  (Wendekreisradius 5 m)
— geringer Benzinverbrauch (ca. 7 Liter / 100 km)
— hohe Reisegeschwindigkeit (ca. 110 km)
— moderne Form (im Windkanal berechnet)
— gute Sicht (6 Fenster, kurzer Vorbau)
— luftgekühlter Motor (kein Sieden im Sommer, keine Frostschäden im Winter)

11

Gediegene Eleganz

und eine Ausstattung von geschmackvoller Vornehmheit, entworfen von einem der namhaftesten Autoarchitekten, sind die äußeren Kennzeichen des viersitzigen ⓦ Cabriolets.

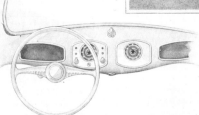

Die begehrte Karosserie

für den begehrtesten deutschen Wagen: das ist das viersitzige ⓦ Cabriolet. Es fügt zu den einzigartigen Vorzügen des Volkswagens die luxuriösen Annehmlichkeiten einer Karosserie, die bei jedem Wetter ein Höchstmaß an Fahrgenuß und Fahrkomfort gewährt.

The first catalog for the four-seat convertible, built by the coachbuilding firm of Karmann in Osnabrück. This model was the ancestor of a long line of constantly improved open Volkswagens, and the car's appearance is quite similar to the last variant of 1980.

Pure Elegance

and equipped with taste and excellence, developed by one of the mo renowned auto architects—the outward signs of the four-seat VW convertible.

The desired body style

for the most desired German car: the four-seat VW convertible. To tl unique advantages of the Volkswagen it adds the luxurious qualiti of a body that assures the highest degree of driving pleasure an comfort in any weather.

Sorgfältig abgestimmte Farbzusammenstellungen

Stilvoll ausgestattetes Armaturenbrett

Modernes, griffiges Zweispeichen-Lenkrad

Erstaunlich viel Raum

für alle Insassen und für großes Reisegepäck ist eines der wesentlichsten Merkmale dieser geglückten Karosseriekonstruktion. Bequem sitzen und fahren 4 erwachsene Personen, behaglich gebettet in sorgsam gearbeitete Polster — ungetrübte Reisefreude auch auf großer Fahrt.

The convertible was delivered with the best series-production interior decor; four people sat in comfort and could enjoy this form of transportation in nice weather.

Carefully chosen color combinations

Stylishly designed dashboard

Modern, easy-to-hold two-spoke steering wheel

Remarkable amount of space

for all passengers and for large travel luggage is one of the mo important characteristics of this body construction. Four grown-people sit and ride in comfort, pleasantly resting on carefully prepar upholstery—untroubled traveling joy even on a long ride.

**VOLKSWAGEN
4 SEATER**

Convertible

Ein echter VOLKSWAGEN

ist auch das viersitzige VW Cabriolet — mit allen Vorzügen, die diese Konstruktion von Weltruf auszeichnen, mit allen Eigenschaften, die Kenner von einem fortschrittlichen Wagen verlangen:

- Der unter allen nur denkbaren Betriebsverhältnissen bewährte luftgekühlte Motor
- Extrem niedriger Verbrauch — echte 7,5 Liter auf 100 km/h!
- Die hinreißende Bergfreudigkeit (autobahnfest!)
- Die serienmäßige Warmluftheizung
- Das rasante Anzugsvermögen
- Die berühmte VW-Straßenlage

und alle anderen Errungenschaften, die eben den Begriff Volkswagen ausmachen

Druckerei H. Osterwald · Hannover

Right: the originally built 25-hp boxer motor also was economical and did not cause the owner such high fuel expenditures as in later years—the performance figures stated in this brochure are not exaggerated.

A real **Volkswagen**

is also the four-seat VW convertible—with all the advantages that characterize this world-renowned construction, with all the characteristics that connoisseurs expect from a progressive car:

The air-cooled motor, tested under all imaginable operating conditions

Extremely low fuel consumption—under 2 gallons at 62 mph

The intense joy of the mountains (firm on the Autobahn!)

Standard warm-air heating

Speedy pick-up

The famous VW roadholding

And all the achievements that form the Volkswagen concept

At the beginning of the fifties, soft, flowing styles gained popularity, a fact taken into consideration by the auto artist Reuters in this catalog.

Das CABRIOLET

The *Convertible*

Cabriolet

Convertible

TWO CARS IN ONE!

The VW convertible for high demands on equipment. The weathertight, padded top can be opened and closed in seconds (Karmann bodywork).

ZWEI WAGEN IN EINEM!
Das VW-Cabriolet für hohe Ansprüche an die Ausstattung. Das wetterfeste, zugdichte Verdeck läßt sich in Sekunden öffnen und schließen (Karmann-Karosserie)

VW-SONNENDACH, Bild unten, für Standard- und Export-Modell auf Wunsch lieferbar. Während der Fahrt ist es mit einem einzigen Handgriff in jeder Stellung fixierbar (Bauart Golde)

VW SUNROOF
available on request for standard and export models. During the trip it can be fixed in either position with a single move of the hand (Goldebuilt).

The good roadholding and driving security of the VW were improved with a combination of low center of gravity; harmonious weight distribution; light-touch steering and torsion-bar suspension; and recently by the refined, softer suspension of the independently sprung wheels. While the shift-happy and sporty-driving motorist can find what he wants as before in the standard model, the VW driver who thinks first of comfort enjoys in the export model the new synchronized transmission, with which shifting becomes play. The inner and outer appearance of the car has been modernized tastefully and the demand for the highest joy of driving has been met, for example, by effective noise reduction, improved form and springing of the seats, swing-out vent windows on both doors, capable windshield wipers and refined heat regulation. But what stayed the same and was not to be increased is the complete synthesis of performance and economy.

Its amazingly low fuel consumption, unproblematic upkeep and care, maintenance of value, and the advantages of a far-reaching and close-knit service network made the VW the most popular German car. In view of its practicality in traffic and on winding roads, and above all in view of its demands on the pocketbook, it is indeed a "small car." Its quickness, endurance, and performance raise it far above itself: the VW is simply in a "CLASS BY ITSELF." The VW is an automobile for all needs, and holds its gained advantage with assurance!

pumpe. Wenn die gute Straßenlage und Fahrsicherheit des VW als Kombination von tiefer Schwerpunktlage, harmonischer Gewichtsverteilung, leichtgängiger Lenkung und Torsionsstab-Federung überhaupt noch zu steigern war, so neuerdings durch die verfeinerte, weichere Abfederung der einzeln aufgehängten Räder. Während der schaltfreudige und sportlich fahrende Automobilist im Standard-Modell wie bisher auf seine Rechnung kommen kann, genießt der außerdem auf Bequemlichkeit bedachte VW-Fahrer im Export-Modell das neue, synchronisierte Getriebe, mit dem das Schalten zum Spiel wird. Zudem wurde das Erscheinungsbild des Wagens innen wie außen geschmackvoll modernisiert und der Forderung nach höchster Annehmlichkeit des Fahrens, z. B. durch wirkungsvolle Abdämpfung der Geräusche, verbesserte Form und Federung der Sitze, schwenkbare Drehfenster an den beiden Türen,

leistungsfähigere Scheibenwischer und verfeinerte Heizungsregulierung, Rechnung getragen ● Was aber gleich blieb und auch nicht zu steigern war, das ist die vollendete Synthese von Leistung und Wirtschaftlichkeit. Sein verblüffend geringer Kraftstoffverbrauch, seine Anspruchslosigkeit in Unterhalt und Pflege, die Erhaltung seiner Wertbeständigkeit, die Vorteile eines weitgespannten und engmaschigen Kundendienst-Netzes haben den so fahrtüchtigen VW zum populärsten deutschen Automobil gemacht. Hinsichtlich seiner Wendigkeit im Verkehrsgewühl und auf Serpentinen und vor allem auch hinsichtlich seiner Ansprüche an die Brieftasche ist er freilich ein „kleiner Wagen"; seine Schnelligkeit, seine Ausdauer, seine Leistung schlechthin aber heben ihn weit über sich selber hinaus: der VW ist eben eine „KLASSE FÜR SICH", ein Automobil für alle Ansprüche und hält mit Sicherheit den errungenen Vorsprung!

CABRIOLET

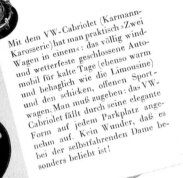

Mit dem VW-Cabriolet (Karmann-Karosserie) hat man praktisch »Zwei Wagen in einem«: das völlig wind- und wetterfeste geschlossene Automobil für kalte Tage (ebenso warm und behaglich wie die Limousine) und den schicken, offenen Sportwagen. Man muß zugeben: das VW-Cabriolet fällt durch seine elegante Form auf jedem Parkplatz angenehm auf. Kein Wunder, daß es bei der selbstfahrenden Dame besonders beliebt ist!

With the VW convertible (Karmann bodywork) one has practically "two cars in one": the fully wind- and weathertight closed car for cold days (just as warm and cozy as the sedan) and the chic open sports car. One must admit: the VW convertible attracts attention at any parking place with its elegant form. No wonder that it is especially popular with the self-driving lady!

Auch das Sonnendach (Bauart Golde) hat viele Freunde gewonnen. Geschlossen bietet es vollkommene Geborgenheit; und offen macht es den VW gewissermaßen zu einer windgeschützten Ecke inmitten der Natur. Hinzu kommt: auch bei schneller Fahrt ist das in jeder Stellung fixierbare VW-Sonnendach mit einem Griff leicht zu öffnen und zu schließen

The sunroof too (Golde-built) also has won many friends. Closed, it offers complete privacy; open, it makes the VW more or less an out-of-the-wind corner amid nature. In addition, even while driving fast, the VW sunroof can be fixed in either position and can be opened and closed easily with one move of the hand.

SONNENDACH

Customers who did not want quite so much breeze ordered the VW with a big sunroof; they enjoyed lots of fresh air just the same and saved a lot of money compared to the convertible.

In the central instrument dial you see at a glance whether or not the motor is healthy. Naturally the driver has his own easy chair (each front seat is independently adjustable during a trip). Even larger persons can sit comfortably in the back seat. There is a surprising amount of space in two luggage areas.

Beautiful in form and purposeful is the decor of the VW, as are the arrangement and formation of all important interior details. The harmony and assortment of the colors are very pleasant; just feel how soft the upholstery is, how naturally you sit!

Volkswagen drivers often take long trips. The VW makes them effortless with the top speed of 68 mph, which you can hold confidently for hours without any limitation. It also is aided by the secure roadholding, the fast acceleration and, not least, by the view of the road just a short distance in front of the car.

CHASSIS

Low-pressure super-balloon tires bring about the comfortable softness of the ride.

A steering built for sporty driving: it reacts sensitively and quickly.

The front and rear torsion-bar suspension easily absorbs the bumps in the road.

The steel backbone in the center of the protective bottom plate gives the VW its firmness.

Uncommonly well-functioning four-speed transmission.

The air-cooled four-cylinder motor, thrifty and durable, produces 30 hp.

Reserves of performance at all engine speeds.

Soft-acting, reliable and evenly working brakes offer the highest safety.

When this brochure was printed, the power of the rear engine already had been increased to 30 horsepower.

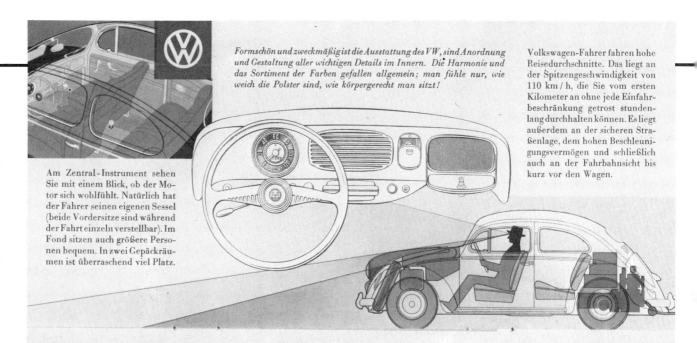

Formschön und zweckmäßig ist die Ausstattung des VW, sind Anordnung und Gestaltung aller wichtigen Details im Innern. Die Harmonie und das Sortiment der Farben gefallen allgemein; man fühle nur, wie weich die Polster sind, wie körpergerecht man sitzt!

Volkswagen-Fahrer fahren hohe Reisedurchschnitte. Das liegt an der Spitzengeschwindigkeit von 110 km / h, die Sie vom ersten Kilometer an ohne jede Einfahrbeschränkung getrost stundenlang durchhalten können. Es liegt außerdem an der sicheren Straßenlage, dem hohen Beschleunigungsvermögen und schließlich auch an der Fahrbahnsicht bis kurz vor den Wagen.

Am Zentral-Instrument sehen Sie mit einem Blick, ob der Motor sich wohlfühlt. Natürlich hat der Fahrer seinen eigenen Sessel (beide Vordersitze sind während der Fahrt einzeln verstellbar). Im Fond sitzen auch größere Personen bequem. In zwei Gepäckräumen ist überraschend viel Platz.

FAHRGESTELL

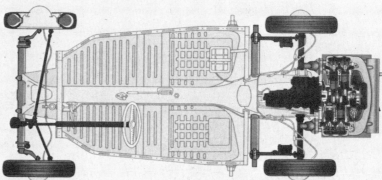

Niederdruck-Superballon-reifen bewirken die wohltuende Weichheit des Fahrens

Eine Lenkung, geschaffen für sportliches Fahren: sie reagiert fein mit kurzem Einschlag

Ungemein günstig übersetztes Viergang-Getriebe

Der luftgekühlte 4-Zylinder-Boxermotor, sparsam und unverwüstlich, leistet 30 PS

Leistungsreserve in allen Drehzahlbereichen

Die Drehstab-Federung vorn und hinten schluckt leicht die Stöße der Fahrbahn

Das stählerne Rückgrat inmitten der schützenden Bodenplatte gibt dem VW die Festigkeit

Sanft angreifende, zuverlässig und gleichmäßig wirkende Bremsen bieten höchste Sicherheit

Über

den

Der Ruf des Volkswagenwerkes und seiner Erzeugnisse ist in wenigen Jahren über alle Länder und Meere gedrungen. In der Tat gibt es im Jahrhundert der Motorisierung eine absolute Garantie für Qualität und Preiswürdigkeit eines Automobils nur auf der Basis der summierten Erfahrungs- und Rationalitätswerte einer großfabrikatorischen Fließbandfertigung. Hier nur können sich weitblickende Konstruktionsgedanken mit modernsten Produktionsmethoden und einer unerbittlichen Kontrolle aller Materialien und Arbeitsvorgänge zu höchster Leistung vereinigen. Diese Voraussetzungen sind in Wolfsburgs hochmodernen und vielbesuchten Produktionsstätten bereits zur stolzen Tradition geworden. Über das hier produzierte, meistgekaufte deutsche Automobil hat die Masse der Käufer selbst — auch in automobilistisch sehr verwöhnten Ländern — ein begeistertes Urteil gefällt, das durch den Kaufentschluß und die Treue Hunderttausender von VW-Fahrern stets aufs neue bestätigt wird.

So ist der einzigartige Siegeslauf des Volkswagens einer überragenden technischen Grundkonzeption ebenso zu verdanken wie den Hunderten von technischen Neuerungen, mit denen der VW seither sich selber treu geblieben ist und im Sinne kühnen Fortschritts dennoch ständig verjüngt wurde. In ihm ist alles vereint, was unermüdlicher Forschung und jahrelanger Erfahrung standhielt:

Der strapazierfähige VW-Heck-Motor von höchster Lebensdauer und großer Kraftreserve, dessen Luftkühlung mit automatischer Regulierung schon längst als hervorragende Lösung des Kühlproblems anerkannt ist,

zeichnet sich durch seine in fortlaufender Weiterentwicklung gesteigerte Leistung und Elastizität aus. Als Kombination von günstiger Schwerpunktlage, harmonischer Gewichtsverteilung, direkter Lenkung, geschmeidiger Torsionsstab-Federung und einzeln aufgehängten Rädern sind Straßenlage und Fahrsicherheit zur Vollendung geführt. Ohne Konzessionen gegenüber unnützen Modeerscheinungen entspricht das Erscheinungsbild des Wagens innen wie außen einem sehr anspruchsvollen Geschmack und auch der Forderung nach hoher Annehmlichkeit des Fahrens.

Was den VW aber besonders auszeichnet, das ist die einmalig geglückte Synthese von Leistung und Wirtschaftlichkeit. Sein verblüffend geringer Kraftstoffverbrauch, seine Anspruchslosigkeit in Unterhalt und Pflege, die Erhaltung seines hohen Wertes auch nach Zehntausenden von Kilometern, die Vorteile einer engmaschigen und weitverzweigten Kundendienst-Organisation haben den VW zum populärsten deutschen Automobil gemacht und ihm in der ganzen Welt einen Rang gegeben, der seinesgleichen sucht. Hinsichtlich seiner Ansprüche an die Brieftasche und seiner Wendigkeit im Verkehrsgewühl und auf steilsten Alpenstraßen ist er freilich ein „kleiner Wagen"; bezüglich seiner hohen Geschwindigkeit, seiner Ausdauer, seiner Leistung schlechthin aber nimmt er es leicht mit vielen Wagen doppelter Größe und doppelten Preises auf. Der VW ist eine „KLASSE FÜR SICH", ein Automobil für höchste Ansprüche und deshalb genau der richtige Wagen für ein Publikum, das auf wirtschaftliche Vernunft ebenso bedacht ist wie auf technischen Fortschritt.

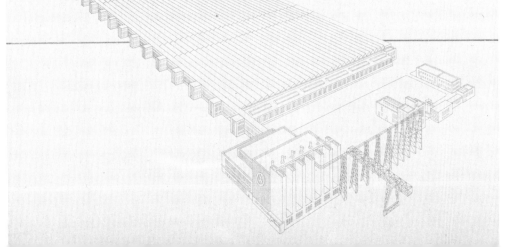

The Assembly Line by the Midland Canal

The reputation of the Volkswagen factory and its products has spread over all lands and seas in a few years. In the century of motoring, there is an absolute guarantee of an automobile's quality and economy only on the basis of the cumulative values of the experience and rationality of large-factory assembly-line manufacture. Only here can far-seeing construction concepts unite with the most modern production methods and a strict control of all materials and work processes to give the highest achievement. These demands already have become a proud tradition in Wolfsburg's highly modern and often-visited production sites. About the best-selling German car, which is built here, the masses of buyers themselves—even here in a land very accustomed to good cars—have expressed an enthusiastic verdict, which is verified anew constantly by the buying decisions and the loyalty of hundreds of thousands of VW drivers.

Thus the unique triumph of the Volkswagen is caused by an outstanding technical basic concept plus the hundreds of technical advances with which the VW since has remained true to itself and has been kept young constantly in the sense of bold progress. Everything is united in it that tireless progress and years of experience have maintained.

The durable VW rear engine is of highest endurance and greatest power reserves. It stands out with its power and flexibility, which have been increased through constant further development. The VW's air cooling with automatic regulation long has been recognized as an outstanding solution of the cooling problem. As a combination of a favorable center of gravity, harmonious weight distribution, direct steering, excellent torsion-bar suspension and independently sprung wheels, its roadholding and driving safety have been perfected. Without concessions to useless fashion fads, the appearance of the car inside and out represents very discriminating taste as well as the advance of high driving pleasure.

But what makes the VW stand out is the uniquely successful synthesis of performance and economy. Its amazingly low fuel consumption, minimal needs in service and care, maintenance of value even after tens of thousands of miles, and the advantages of a close-knit and widespread network of service agencies all have made the VW the most popular German car and given it unequaled status in the world. In view of its low demands on the pocketbook and its handiness in traffic or on the steepest Alpine roads, it is indeed a "small car." But when it comes to its high speed, durability, and performance, it compares with many cars twice its size and twice its cost. The VW is in a "CLASS BY ITSELF"; an automobile to meet the highest demand; the right car for a public that is just as concerned about economic practicality as about technical progress.

The Volkswagen firm's success increased considerably from year to year. This success was reported in inclusive catalogs which showed what outstanding characteristics of the automobiles from Wolfsburg had contributed to its development.

AN EXPERIENCE

THUS ONE RIDES ON THE FLATLANDS AS IN THE MOUNTAINS, on the Autobahn as on side roads, on business trips as in fulfillment of daring vacation wishes, always well-equipped in a VW—and with justified trust in a network of service agencies that is as widespread as it is finely meshed and stands ready anywhere and anytime with quick service and knowledgeable repairs. As a VW driver one finds a home everywhere: at more than 900 VW specialized agencies in the Federal Republic, at 180 in Switzerland, and at numerous locations in neighboring European countries and overseas. Factory-trained specialists; tested workshop procedures; carefully calculated prices for work; a centrally controlled spare-part supply and a time-tested, practical exchange system for factory-overhauled components make this unique service organization a model of reliability. Economical and time-saving car service, repairs and the fulfilling of special wishes: all this takes the financial risk from the maintenance of an automobile and assures the car's value to its ripe old age to an incomparable degree.

VW SERVICE ANYWHERE AND ANYTIME

A great benefit for people who chose a Volkswagen was the remarkable network of customer service stations, which gave the traveler a feeling of security—even in foreign countries.

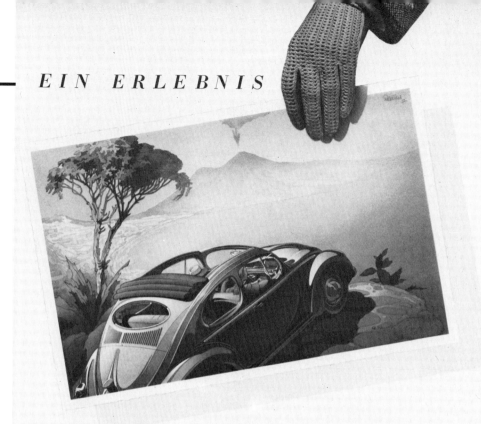

BLICK INS INNERE

DER GENUSS DES FAHRENS beginnt schon, wenn man den Wagen betritt, denn formschön und zweckmäßig ist auch die innere Architektur des VW. Die Cord- (beim Standard-Modell Tuch-) Polsterstoffe wie auch die Tür- und Wandverkleidungen harmonieren in modischen Farben und Mustern mit dem neuen Farbsortiment der Lackierung und den elfenbein (beim Standard-Modell dunkel) gehaltenen Griffknöpfen und Rosetten. Sitze und Lehnen sind hinsichtlich weicher Federung und haltbietender Plastik (Randwülste aus Schaumgummi) geradezu ideal konstruiert. Die Vordersessel sind auch während der Fahrt einzeln verstellbar und haben stärker geneigte Lehnen; die breite Sitzbank im Fond bietet erforderlichenfalls drei Personen Platz, denen durch großen Abstand zwischen Vorder- und Hintersitzen und durch Erweiterung des Fußraumes ausreichende Bewegungsfreiheit geschaffen wurde. Bei Dunkelheit spendet eine im Dachholm links überm Fahrersitz eingebaute Innenleuchte gute Helligkeit, während das angenehme, beliebig regulierbare Flutlicht des Zentralinstruments das Gefühl einer sicheren Geborgenheit noch erhöht. In der ebenso modern-geschmackvollen wie technisch durchdachten Armaturentafel vereinigt sich in handlicher Anordnung lückenlos alles, was zum Fahren notwendig oder nützlich ist:

1. WINKERHEBEL an der Lenksäule, von der linken Hand mit einem Finger zu betätigen

2. Großes ZENTRALINSTRUMENT mit Tachometer, Kilometerzähler und den im Zifferblatt harmonisch eingefügten Kontroll-Leuchten für Lichtmaschine und Kühlung (rot), Öldruck (grün), Fernlicht (blau) und Winker (Doppelpfeil)

3. Sehr ansprechendes, überraschend griffiges ZWEISPEICHEN-LENKRAD, hellfarben getönt, mit schwarz-goldenem, wappengeschmücktem Signalknopf (Export-Modell)

4. Flinke SCHEIBENWISCHER mit weitem Ausschlag und festem Aufdruck, beim Export-Modell mit automatischer Rückkehr in Tiefstellung beim Abschalten

5. Platz für RUNDFUNKSKALA und Bedienungsknöpfe, links daneben ein Zugschalter für Scheibenwischer, ferner ein Dreh-Zugschalter für Scheinwerfer und die feinregulierbare Beleuchtung des Zentralinstruments

6. Hinter geschmackvollem Ziergitter der große Raum für den Einbau eines RADIOGERÄTES

7. Handlich rechts vor dem Fahrer der Zugknopf für die LUFTKLAPPE ALS STARTERHILFE

8. Kombiniertes ZÜND-ANLASS-SCHLOSS; Zündschlüssel ist gleichzeitig auch Türschlüssel

9. Versenkbarer, großer KIPP-ASCHER

10. Schließbarer, geräumiger HANDSCHUHKASTEN

UNMITTELBAR IM BLICKFELD DES FAHRERS liegt das geschmackvoll und übersichtlich eingeteilte Zentralinstrument, das bei Dunkelheit beleuchtet werden kann und in dem alle während der Fahrt zu überwachenden Kontrollorgane zusammengefaßt sind.

1310 mm
51.6 inch

A LOOK INSIDE

THE JOY OF DRIVING already begins when one enters the because the interior design of the VW is beautiful and practical. corduroy (or cloth in the standard model) upholstery fabrics, like door and wall coverings, harmonize in fashionable colors and patt with the new body colors and the ivory (dark in the standard mo handles, knobs and rosettes. Seats and backs are ideally constru with soft springs and durable plastic (with foam rubber edgings). front seats also are adjustable independently in transit and have r strongly tilted backs. The wide bench seat in the back offers spac three people if necessary, for the distance between the front and seats and the expanded foot space offer sufficient freedom of movem In darkness an interior light, located at the left edge of the roof ove driver's seat, provides good light while the pleasant, adjus lighting of the central instrument panel increases the feeling of se coziness. On the dashboard, which is as modern and tasteful as technically designed, everything that is necessary or useful w driving is present in handy positions.

01. DIRECTIONAL SIGNAL LEVER on the steering colu activated with one finger of the left hand.
02. Big CENTRAL INSTRUMENT PANEL with speedom odometer and harmoniously located indicator lights fo generator and cooling (red), oil pressure (green), high b (blue) and directionals (double arrow).
03. Very impressive, surprisingly holdable TWO-SP STEERING WHEEL with black and gold horn button bea the VW coat of arms (export model).
04. Nimble WINDSHIELD WIPER with long reach and pressure; the export model's returns to its bottom position v turned off.
05. Place for RADIO DIAL and operating knobs, nearby to the pull switch for the windshield washer, also a rotating switc the headlights and fine regulation of the dashboard lights.
06. Behind a tasteful grid, a large space for the installation RADIO.
07. Handy at the driver's right is the pull knob for the AIR INT for starting help.
08. Combined IGNITION-ENTRY LOCK: the ignition key is the door key.
09. Large lowerable TIPPING ASHTRAY.
10. Closing, roomy GLOVE COMPARTMENT.

RIGHT IN THE DRIVER'S FIELD OF VISION lies the tastefu easy-to-read central instrument dial, which can be lighted in the and on which all the controls one needs to see are brought toge

Karmann Keeps It Rolling

By the time Hebmüller no longer built convertibles, Wolfsburg itself produced only the sedan. It was up to Karmann to provide the open version of the Volkswagen. The Beetle convertible was the world production champion in its class and became one of the most popular middle-class soft-tops in the world. The last open Karmann Beetle left the Osnabrück plant in January of 1980.

TECHNICAL

MOTOR

...PE:	4-cylinder 4-stroke gasoline engine
...LINDER PATTERN:	Boxer motor with two cylinders each, horizontally opposed
...LVES:	Dropped
...LINDER BORE:	77 mm
...ROKE:	64 mm
...PLACEMENT:	1192 cc
...MPRESSION RATIO:	6.6 : 1
...RSEPOWER:	30 hp at 3400 rpm
...TON SPEED:	7.25 m/s at 3400 rpm '68 mph
...BRICATION:	Pressure circulation (gear-driven fuel pump) with oil cooler
...CAPACITY:	2.5 quarts
...EL PUMP:	Mechanical
...RBURETOR:	Downdraft with accelerator pump: Solex 28 PCI
...FILTER:	Oil-bath filter
...OLING:	Air-cooled by blower, automatically regulated by thermostat
...TTERY:	6-Volt, 70 Ah
...RTER:	Pusher-screw drive, made by Bosch
...NERATOR:	Tension-regulated 160-watt, made by **Bosch**

CLUTCH

...nual dry coupling

GEARS

...ort Model and Convertible
...NSTRUCTION: Indirect 4-speed drive, 2nd, 3rd and 4th gears synchronized

...AR RATIOS: 1st: 1:3.60, 2nd: 1:1.88, 3rd: 1:1.23, 4th: 1:0.82; Reverse: 1:4.63

...dard Model
...NSTRUCTION: Indirect 4-speed drive, 3rd and 4th gears synchronized

...AR RATIOS: 1st: 1:3.60, 2nd: 1:2.07, 3rd: 1:1.25, 4th: 1:0.80; Reverse: 1:6.60

REAR AXLE

...WER TRANSMISSION: By spiral bevel-wheel drive, differential and swing axles to the rear wheels.

...TIO: 1:4.4
... CAPACITY: Differential and rear axle: 2.5 quarts
At oil change: 2 quarts

CHASSIS

...NSTRUCTION: Central pipe frame with rear fork and welded platform
...ONT AXLE: Independent suspension by upper and lower longitudinal links: two transverse leaf springs protected by casings
...AR AXLE: Independent suspension by swing half-axles with longitudinal links: one torsion bar on each side, built into the frame's transverse tube
...OCK ABSORBERS: Maintenance-free front and rear hydraulic telescopic double-action shock absorbers
...ERING: Special spindle steering with divided rack, 2.4 turns of the steering wheel from contact to contact
...RNING CIRCLE: Approximately 36 feet
...ES: 560-15
...EELS: Disc wheels with deep-bed rims, 4J x 15
...KES: *Export model and convertible:* Hydraulic foot brake (Ate) working on 4 wheels; mechanical hand brake working on rear wheels
Standard model: Mechanical foot and hand brakes, both working on all 4 wheels
...EELBASE: 2400 mm
...ACK: Front 1290 mm, rear 1250 mm
...L TANK: 10.5 gallons, including 5-quart reserve

OVERALL DIMENSIONS

Length 13.35 feet, width 5 feet, height 4.9 feet

WEIGHT in lbs.

	Sedan	Convertible
net weight:	1562	1716
dry weight:	1616	1760
load limit:	836	792
allowable gross weight:	2442	2552

PERFORMANCE

FUEL CONSUMPTION: 7 quarts per 62 miles by German norms; Average consumption 7 quarts per 62 miles

SPEEDS: Top and cruising speed 68 mph

CLIMBING ABILITY:
1st gear 37%,
2nd 18.5%,
3rd 11%,
4th 6% (Data according to VDA and German Industrial Norms)

ADDITIONAL DETAILS: Draft-free all-steel body with highly polished weathertight synthetic resin finish—Interior sound-solated from motor compartment-continuous metallic trim on both sides-tipping ashtray in rear-door pocket near driver's seat (export model)—left nterior light over driver's seat-rubber floor mats-luggage space behind the rear seat and under the front hood

As the whole car, so too did the dashboard undergo steady changes and improvements in many details. This dashboard of the mid-fifties no longer had anything in common with the first version.

MOTOR

BAUART	4-Zylinder-4-Takt-Vergasermotor
ZYLINDERANORDNUNG	je 2 Zylinder gegenüberliegend — Boxermotor
VENTILE	hängend
ZYLINDERBOHRUNG	77 mm
KOLBENHUB	64 mm
HUBRAUM	1192 cm³
VERDICHTUNGSVERHÄLTNIS	6,6
HÖCHSTLEISTUNG	30 PS bei 3400 U/min
KOLBENGESCHWINDIGKEIT	7,25 m/s bei 3400 U/min = 110 km/h
SCHMIERUNG	Druckumlaufschmierung (Zahnradpumpe) mit Ölkühler
ÖLINHALT	2,5 l
KRAFTSTOFF-FÖRDERUNG	mechan. Kraftstoffpumpe
VERGASER	Fallstromvergaser mit Beschleunigungspumpe SOLEX 28 PCI
LUFTFILTER	Ölbadfilter
KÜHLUNG	Luftkühlung durch Gebläse, automatisch durch Thermostat geregelt
BATTERIE	6 V, 70 Ah
ANLASSER	Schubschraubtrieb-Anlasser Fabrikat Bosch
LICHTMASCHINE	spannungsregelnd Bosch, Leistung 160 Watt

KUPPLUNG

Einscheiben-Trockenkupplung

GETRIEBE

Export-Modell und Cabriolet
BAUART: Indirektes Vierganggetriebe. 2., 3. und 4. Gang sperrsynchronisiert

ÜBERSETZUNGSVERHÄLTNIS:
1. Gang 1:3,60 2. Gang 1:1,88
3. Gang 1:1,23 4. Gang 1:0,82
Rückwärtsgang 1:4,63

Standard-Modell
BAUART: Indirektes Vierganggetriebe. 3. und 4. Gang geräuscharm

ÜBERSETZUNGSVERHÄLTNIS:
1. Gang 1:3,60 2. Gang 1:2,07
3. Gang 1:1,25 4. Gang 1:0,80
Rückwärtsgang 1:6,60

HINTERACHSE

KRAFTÜBERTRAGUNG: durch spiralverzahntes Kegelradgetriebe, Kegelradausgleichgetriebe und Pendelachsen auf die Hinterräder

ÜBERSETZUNGSVERHÄLTNIS: 1:4,4

ÖLINHALT: von Getriebe und Hinterachse 2,5 l Füllmenge bei Ölwechsel 2,0 l

FAHRGESTELL

BAUWEISE	Zentralrohrrahmen mit hinterer Gabel und angeschweißter Plattform
VORDERACHSE	Einzelradaufhängung durch Längslenker oben und unten; 2 lamellierte, querliegende, in Tragrohren geschützte Drehfederstäbe
HINTERACHSE	Einzelradaufhängung durch Pendel-Halbachsen mit Längslenkern; ein Drehfederstab auf jeder Seite, geschützt im Rahmenquerrohr eingebaut
STOSSDÄMPFER	vorn und hinten wartungsfreie hydraulische Teleskop-Stoßdämpfer, doppeltwirkend
LENKUNG	Spezial-Spindel-Lenkung mit geteilter Spurstange. 2,4 Lenkradumdrehungen von Anschlag zu Anschlag
WENDEKREIS	etwa 11 m
BEREIFUNG	5,60 — 15
RÄDER	Scheibenräder mit Tiefbettfelge 4 J × 15
BREMSEN	*Export-Modell und Cabriolet* Fußbremse hydraulisch (Ate), auf 4 Räder wirkend; Handbremse mechanisch, auf die Hinterräder wirkend *Standard-Modell* Fuß- und Handbremse mechanisch, auf alle 4 Räder wirkend
RADSTAND	2400 mm
SPURWEITE	vorn 1290 mm hinten 1250 mm
KRAFTSTOFFBEHÄLTER	40 l, davon 5 l Reserve

ABMESSUNGEN ÜBER ALLES

Länge: 4070 mm   Breite: 1540 mm
Höhe: 1500 mm

GEWICHT IN kg

	Limousine	Cabriolet
Eigengewicht	710	780
Leergewicht	730	800
Nutzlast	380	360
Zul. Gesamtgewicht	1110	1160

FAHRLEISTUNGEN

KRAFTSTOFFVERBRAUCH: Normverbrauch 6,5 l/100 km Durchschnittsverbrauch 7,5 l/100 km

GESCHWINDIGKEITEN: Dauer- und Höchstgeschwindigkeit 110 km/h

STEIGFÄHIGKEIT:
1. Gang 37 %   3. Gang 11 %
2. Gang 18,5 %   4. Gang 6 %

Laut VDA-Revers technische Angaben entsprechend DIN 70020 und DIN 70030

WEITERE EINZELHEITEN: Verwindungssteife Ganzstahlkarosserie mit hochglänzender, wetterfester Kunstharzlackierung • Geräusch-Isolierung des Wageninnern gegen den Motorraum • Durchlaufende Zierleisten auf beiden Innenseiten; eingebauter Kipp-Ascher im Fond; Türtasche neben dem Fahrersitz (Export-Modell) • Innenbeleuchtung links über dem Fahrersitz • Gummi-Fußmatten • Gepäckraum hinter den Rücksitzen und unter der vorderen Haube

The VW is "Tops"!

In the fifties and sixties, "paintings" full of atmosphere still graced the title pages of sales catalogs. Originally meant to lure buyers, they are now a source of pleasure to people with a feeling for nostalgia.

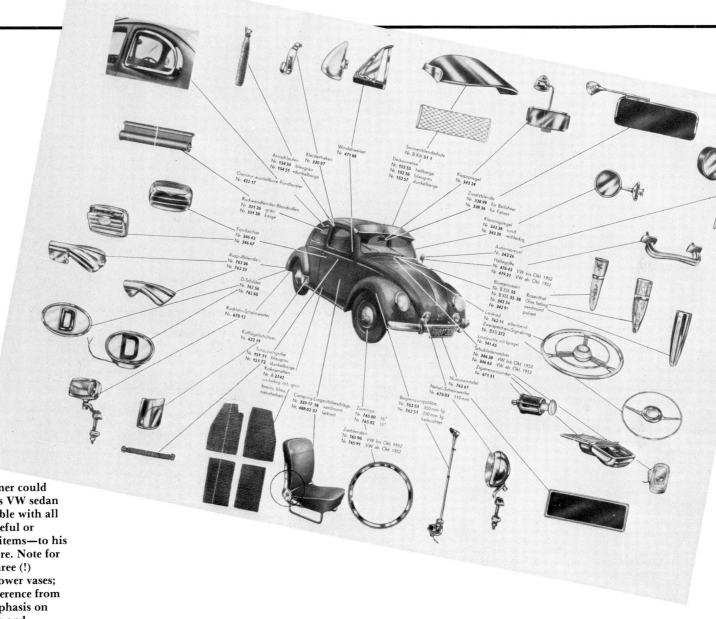

parts clockwise from top

Outside sun visor

Covering nets
light tan, blue-gray, dark tan

Adjustable mirror

Sun visor
for passenger, for driver

Screw-on mirror
round, square

Outside mirror

Handhold
until October 1952, as of October 1952

Flower vases
Rosenthal, tinted glass, chromed, polished

Steering wheel
ivory, two-spoked, horn ring

Reading light with mirror

Pull-out ashtray

Cigarette lighter

Number plate

Fog light

Curb finder
350 mm long, 350 mm long with light

Decorative wheel ring
decorative cover: until October 1952,
as of October 1952

Camping lie-down seat
chromed, painted

Floor mat
solid red, green
brown, blue, natural color

Door grip
blue-gray, dark tan

Fender guard

Back-up light

National shield

Exhaust shield

Rear ashtray

Rear window blind

Opening rear window

Hanging strap
blue-gray, dark tan

Coat hook

Vent window

Any customer could ennoble his VW sedan or convertible with all kinds of useful or decorative items—to his heart's desire. Note for example three (!) different flower vases; what a difference from today's emphasis on horsepower and electronics!

23

Cabriolet

Whether in closed or open form, the Beetle was a car of unchanging functional beauty. The top was of outstanding quality and did not make a drafty and cold container of the car, even in winter, about which drivers of other convertibles often could sing the blues.

Wer viel Sonne und Luft während der Fahrt liebt und zugleich hohe Ansprüche an die Ausstattung stellt, findet im VW-CABRIOLET den eleganten Wagen mit allen VW-Vorzügen und einem wetterfesten, zugdichten Verdeck, das sich bequem in Sekunden öffnen und schließen läßt. Durch eine besonders gediegene Ausstattung, die dem verwöhntesten Geschmack Rechnung trägt, wird ein Maximum an Fahrtkomfort und Reisegenuß geboten. Der Käufer hat die Wahl zwischen vielen sorgfältig aufeinander abgestimmten Farbkombinationen, die die individuelle Note des Wagens, seine zeitlos schöne Linie und Form, wirkungsvoll betonen. Dem noblen Stil sind die reichen Chromverzierungen und hochglanzpolierten Schmuckleisten harmonisch angepaßt. Starke, widerstandsfähige Hochglanz-Metallecken schützen die hinteren Kotflügel. Zum serienmäßig gelieferten Zubehör gehören unter anderem auch eine zweite Sonnenblende vor dem Beifahrersitz und ein verchromter Haltegriff über dem verschließbaren großen Handschuhkasten. Exklusive Sonderwünsche jeder Art sind bei entsprechendem Aufpreis leicht erfüllbar. So vereinigen sich im Volkswagen-Cabriolet solide Eleganz und wohldurchdachte Zweckmäßigkeit, technischer Fortschritt und wirtschaftliche Vernunft zu einer erstaunlich guten Lösung. In doppelter Hinsicht stellt es eigentlich „ZWEI WAGEN IN EINEM" dar: offen, mit völlig versenkten Seitenteilen, ist dieses kompromißlose Voll-Cabriolet ein echter Sportkamerad für naturliebende Automobilisten. Geschlossen bietet das dickwattierte, geräuschverzehrende Falt-Verdeck mit seinem jetzt noch fast um die Hälfte vergrößerten Heckfenster die gleiche Geborgenheit, den gleichen Schutz gegen Staub, Wind und Wetter wie das Stahldach der Limousine. Dieser Wagen ist außerdem ein anspruchsloser, zuverlässig treuer Berufsgefährte und zugleich ein vielseitiges, sehr repräsentatives Automobil, das deshalb nicht zuletzt auch von der selbstfahrenden Dame besonders geschätzt wird. Wo immer sich schöne Wagen ansammeln; das VW-Cabriolet findet uneingeschränkte Anerkennung, allgemeine Bewunderung und manchen begehrenden Blick.

Convertible

Whoever loves lots of sun and air during a trip and at the same time expects much of the car's equipment finds in the VW convertible an elegant car with all the VW advantages and a weathertight, airtight top that can be opened and closed easily in seconds. Through a particularly fine furnishing that takes the most pampered tastes into consideration, a maximum of traveling comfort and enjoyment is offered. The buyer has a choice of many carefully chosen color combinations that effectively stress the individual spirit of the car, its timelessly beautiful lines and form. The rich chrome trim and highly polished decorations harmonize with the noble style. Strong, durable highly polished metal corners protect the rear fenders. Among other things, standard equipment includes a second sun visor before the passenger seat and a chromed handhold over the large, locking glove compartment. Exclusive special wishes of every kind easily are obtained at appropriate prices. Thus solid elegance and well-designed practicality, technical progress and economical good sense are united in the Volkswagen convertible in an amazingly good combination.

In two ways it really forms "TWO CARS IN ONE": open, with fully lowering side pieces, this uncompromising full convertible is a true sporting comrade for nature-loving motorists. Closed, the thickly padded, sound-absorbing folding top, with its rear window now enlarged almost by half, offers the same coziness and protection from dust, wind and weather as the steel roof of the sedan.

This car is an undemanding, reliable business vehicle and at the same time a versatile and representative automobile that is particularly valued by the lady who drives herself. Wherever beautiful cars gather, the VW convertible finds unlimited recognition, general admiration and many a desiring glance.

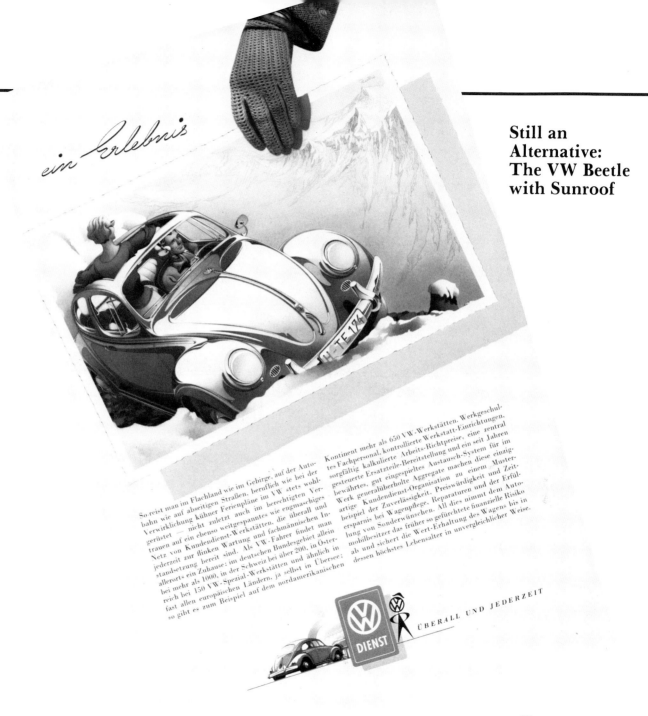

ein Erlebnis

an Experience

text identical to that on page 19

So reist man im Flachland wie im Gebirge, auf der Autobahn wie auf abseitigen Straßen, beruflich wie bei der
Verwirklichung kühner Ferienpläne im VW stets wohl-
gerüstet — nicht zuletzt auch im berechtigten Vertrauen auf ein ebenso weitgespanntes wie engmaschiges
Netz von Kundendienst-Werkstätten, die überall und
jederzeit zur flinken Wartung und fachmännischen Instandsetzung bereit sind. Als VW-Fahrer findet man
allerorts ein Zuhause; im deutschen Bundesgebiet allein
bei mehr als 1000, in der Schweiz bei über 200, in Österreich bei 150 VW-Spezial-Werkstätten und ähnlich in
fast allen europäischen Ländern, ja selbst in Übersee:
so gibt es zum Beispiel auf dem nordamerikanischen

Kontinent mehr als 650 VW-Werkstätten, Werkgeschultes Fachpersonal, kontrollierte Werkstatt-Einrichtungen,
sorgfältig kalkulierte Arbeits-Richtpreise, eine zentral
gesteuerte Ersatzteile-Bereitstellung und ein seit Jahren
bewährtes, gut eingespieltes Austausch-System für im
Werk generalüberholte Aggregate machen diese einzigartige Kundendienst-Organisation zu einem Musterbeispiel der Zuverlässigkeit, Preiswürdigkeit und Zeitersparnis bei Wagenpflege, Reparaturen und der Erfüllung von Sonderwünschen. All dies nimmt dem Auto-
mobilbesitzer das früher so gefürchtete finanzielle Risiko
ab und sichert die Wert-Erhaltung des Wagens bis in
dessen höchstes Lebensalter in unvergleichlicher Weise.

VW DIENST · ÜBERALL UND JEDERZEIT

Motor

B. MÖLLER·56

The four-cylinder boxer motor, proved by a million examples, is shown here in very visible graphics of 1956. Characteristic of the rear end of the Beetle are the two exhaust pipes, introduced in August of 1955.

MOTOR Der ungemein stabile Rahmen-Unterbau trägt im Heck den berühmten, in nahezu, zwei Millionen Exemplaren bewährten VW-Motor. Er ist ein luftgekühlter Vierzylinder-Viertakt-Boxer mit hängenden Ventilen, der am Triebwerkgehäuse, das seinerseits gegen den Wagen isoliert wurde, frei schwebend angeflanscht ist. Je zwei Zylinder liegen sich waagerecht gegenüber, wodurch niedrige Schwerpunktlage und beste Raumnutzung erzielt werden. Als typischer Kurzhuber hat er besonders niedrige Kolbengeschwindigkeiten; daraus erklären sich sein ganz ungewöhnlich geringer Verschleiß, seine absolute Autobahn-Ausdauer und seine sprichwörtliche Langlebigkeit. Die Kurbelwelle dieses Motors ist vierfach gelagert, aus Mangan-Stahl im Gesenk geschmiedet, dynamisch ausgewuchtet und an den Lagerstellen gehärtet. Auf der Kurbelwelle sind die Pleuel in Bleibronzelagern gebettet. Motor, Getriebe, Differential und Hinterachse bilden einen einzigen, organisch gefügten Block, mit dem Ergebnis einer beachtlichen Raum- und Gewichtsersparnis und einer bequem zugänglichen Anordnung an günstigem Platz. Ein Solex-Fallstrom-Vergaser mit Beschleunigungspumpe sichert gute Übergänge, temperamentvolle Beschleunigung, geringen Verbrauch und hohe Elastizität des Motors. Auch bei extrem niedrigen Temperaturen springt der Motor sicher an; die Kaltstart-Luftklappe ist mit der Drosselklappe zur progressiven Leerlauferhöhung gekoppelt. Der VW-Motor kennt keine Einfahrvorschrift. Man kann ihn vom ersten Kilometer an unbedenklich bis zur Höchstgeschwindigkeit ausfahren. Dies verdankt er der laufenden Verfeinerung automobilistischer Produktionstechnik.

MOTOR

The unusually stable frame construction carries the fam VW motor, already tested in nearly two million examples, in the r It is an air-cooled four-cylinder four-stroke boxer with dropped va flexibly mounted in the engine compartment, which is in turn isol from the interior. The two pairs of cylinders are horizontally oppo to each other, achieving a low center of gravity and the best sp utilization. As a typical short-stroke motor, it has particularly l piston speeds, which explains its unusually low friction, absolut long life at Autobahn speed and proverbial durability. The cranksh of the motor has four bearings, is forged of mangan-steel, dynamically balanced and hardened at the bearing points. The pis rods are attached to the crankshaft by lead-bronze bearings. Mot gears, differential and rear axle form a single organically united bl with the result of considerable space and weight saving an convenient arrangement in an accessible place. A Solex downdr carburetor with an accelerator pump assures good transition, spir acceleration, low consumption and high flexibility for the mo Even in extremely low temperatures the motor starts dependably; cold-start choke is linked with the throttle valve for progressi increased idling speed. The VW motor does not need to be broken You can drive it at top speed from the first mile without concern owes this to the ongoing refinement of automobile producti technology.

As an elegant version of the VW Beetle, the convertible had numerous special features for particularly discriminating customers, including such seemingly old-fashioned items as special armrests for the rear passengers.

Impressive special wishes—easily fulfilled

Many nice and useful details to your personal taste at appropriate additional prices

Special traveling inset, useful as either a rear seat or luggage space
Lighted clock left of the instrument panel

Whitewall tires, highly polished metal rims

Snap-on protective cover for steering wheel and rear, including luggage space

Armrest cushions in style and color of the upholstery

Famous auto illustrator Ernst Reuters created numerous beautiful illustrations for VW sales brochures, like this pretty title-page picture.

27

Das VW Cabriolet

Es sind gewiß nicht die schlechtesten Kenner des Automobils, denen es auf sportliches Fahren im offenen Wagen, in Luft und Sonne ankommt, die neben technischen Ansprüchen auch noch hinsichtlich des Komforts besondere Wünsche haben, die ein Auto von eigener Note erstreben und in ihm die Merkmale des individuellen Geschmacks erkennen wollen. Für diese Feinschmecker der Automobiltechnik, ganz speziell, ist das Voll-Cabriolet des Volkswagenwerks die richtige Wahl. Dieser kompromißlose Repräsentant vollendeten Fahrgenusses ist keine halbe Lösung, sondern ein echtes, wirklich offenes Cabriolet mit völlig versenkbaren Seitenteilen, voller Kostbarkeiten in der serienmäßigen Ausstattung und wie geschaffen für anspruchsvolle Sonderwünsche, die leicht erfüllbar sind, weil der Konstrukteur sie voraussah. Im reich komplettierten VW-Cabriolet mit Karmann-Karosserie haben sich technischer Fortschritt und wirtschaftliche Vernunft, wohldurchdachte Zweckmäßigkeit und gediegene Eleganz zu einer erstaunlich guten Lösung vereinigt.

Fahrer und Mitreisende lehnen behaglich in körpergerecht geformten Sitzen. Die Vordersessel wurden verbreitert; sie können beliebig nach vorn oder hinten gerückt und gleichzeitig auch in ihrer Höhenlage verändert werden; die Lehnen sind in drei Neigungsstufen während der Fahrt verstellbar; hochgepolsterte Wulstränder bieten festen seitlichen Halt. Alle Insassen finden - bei vergrößertem Abstand zwischen Vorderlehne und Rückbank - bequem Platz - und mit ihnen das große Reisegepäck, für das auch unter der Vorderhaube nunmehr ein koffergerechtes zweites Depot geschaffen wurde • Viele schöne, sorgfältig ausgewählte Farbkombinationen (Kunstharz-Lackierung), zudem erweiterte Farbskala zur Erfüllung exklusiver Sonderwünsche. Jedes VW-Cabriolet mit individueller Note.

Reiche Chromverzierung, hochglanzpolierte Metall-Leisten. Seitenscheiben eingefaßt. Hochglanz-Metallecken zum Schutz der hinteren Kotflügel, verchromte Auspuffrohre • Kraftvoll im Start - ausdauernd auf der Autobahn, stark in den Bergen - durch den berühmten Volkswagen-Motor! Schnell auf freier Strecke, wendig und sicher im dichtesten Verkehr. Handlich besonders für die Dame durch das bequem zu schaltende Synchron-Getriebe • Spielend leichte Lenkung, weiche, ebenso sanft wie fest greifende Öldruck-Bremse. Hervorragende Straßenlage durch tiefen Schwerpunkt. Progressive Drehstab-Federung, doppeltwirkende Teleskop-Stoßdämpfer und Einzelrad-Aufhängung. Absolute Sicherheit auf kurvenreicher, selbst regennasser Fahrbahn • Dick wattiertes Verdeck, robust und haltbar, gibt Schutz, Zugfreiheit und Wärme. Mit einer Hand zu öffnen - halbautomatisch zusammengefaltet, wird es von einer paspelierten Hülle faltenlos umschlossen • Fein regulierbare Heizung. Warmluft-Frontscheiben-Entfroster. Rasches Spiel der Scheibenwischer, die auf Knopfdruck automatisch in die Ausgangsstellung zurückkehren • Übersichtliches Zentral-instrument, durch Flutlicht beliebig gedämpft beleuchtet. Harmonisch gefügte Armaturentafel mit elfenbeinfarbenen Bedienungsknöpfen und verchromtem Radiogitter. Verschließbarer Handschuhkasten, große Türtaschen an beiden Seiten, elegantes, griffiges Zweispeichen-Lenkrad • Zwei Sonnen-blenden, vibrationsfreier Rückblickspiegel. Für den Beifahrer Armlehne und Haltegriff. Aschenbecher vorn und hinten.

The convertible

It certainly is not those who don't know cars who enjoy driving open cars in fresh air and sunshine, who have special wishes in terms of comfort as well as technical standards, and who want a car with own style that suits their individual tastes. For these gourmets automotive technology, the full convertible from the Volkswagen factory is the right choice. This uncompromising representative of perfect driving pleasure is not a half-solution but a true, open convertible with fully lowering side pieces. The VW is full of value in standard production and features impressive special wishes that are easily fulfilled, because the constructors anticipated them. In the richly appointed VW convertible with body by Karmann, technical progress and economic good sense, well-planned practicality and perfect elegance have been blended remarkably well.

Driver and passengers lean back comfortably in proper proportioned seats. The front seats have been widened; they can be moved forward or back as you wish and also adjust in height. The seat can be adjusted to three degrees of inclination in transit; thick padded edges give firm lateral support. With increased space between the front and rear seats, all occupants find comfortable room—all with room for luggage, for which there is a second luggage area under the front hood. There are many pleasant, carefully selected color combinations (in synthetic resin finish), plus an expanded choice of colors to fulfill exclusive wishes. Every VW convertible has an individual spirit.

Rich chrome trim and highly polished metal side bars are attached. Highly polished metal corners protect the rear fenders and chrome exhaust pipes. Powerful starting—enduring on the Autobahn, strong in the mountains—thanks to the famous Volkswagen motor! Fast on the open road, nimble and sure in the heaviest traffic. Especially handy for the ladies because of the easy-to-shift synchronized gears; playfully easy steering; and soft oleopneumatic brakes, as gentle as they are firm. Outstanding roadholding thanks to a low center of gravity. Progressive torsion-bar suspension, double-acting telescopic shock absorbers and independent suspension. Absolute security on winding, even rain-slick roads. Thickly padded top, robust and durable, gives draft-protection and warmth and can be opened with one hand. The top is semi-automatic folding and is enclosed in a wrinkle-free piping-edged cover. Finely-adjustable heating. Warm-air windshield defroster. Fast-moving windshield wipers that automatically return to their rest position when turned off. Easy-to-see central instrument panel with adjustable lighting. Harmoniously designed dashboard with ivory colored knobs and chromed radio grid. Locking glove compartment, large door pockets on both sides, elegant, holdable two-spoke steering wheel. Two sun visors, vibration-free rear-view mirror. Armrest and handhold for the passenger. Front and rear ashtrays.

The one disadvantage caused by rear-engine construction: the difficult matter of luggage space!

VW

Ein Wagen von besonderer Note — dabei ein echter VW!

Automobile exklusiver Art sind nicht selten ein technisches Wagnis, weil die große Serien-Erprobung fehlt. Beim VW-Cabriolet, so geschmacklich erlesen es ist, so sehr es manch begehrlichen Blick auf sich zieht, so sehr es durch viele nette und nützliche Ausstattungs-Details auf das Niveau eines Kleinods unter den modernen Automobilen gehoben wird, entfällt dieses Risiko: hier verfügt der Fahrer ungeschmälert über alle VW-Werte, die den Volkswagen in millionenfacher Bewährung und stetiger Fortentwicklung in aller Welt berühmt und begehrt gemacht haben.

Motor	Luftgekühlter 4-Zylinder-4-Takt-Boxermotor im Heck, Zylinderbohrung 77 mm, Kolbenhub 64 mm, Hubraum 1192 ccm, 30 PS bei 3400 U/min, Verdichtungsverhältnis 6,6, Ventile hängend
Vergaser	Fallstromvergaser mit Beschleunigungspumpe
Kühlung	Luftkühlung durch Gebläse, automatisch durch Thermostat geregelt
Schmierung	Druckumlaufschmierung mit Ölkühler im Gebläse-Luftstrom
Getriebe Kraftübertragung	2., 3. und 4. Gang sperrsynchronisiert durch spiralverzahntes Kegelradgetriebe, Kegelradausgleichgetriebe und Pendelachsen auf die Hinterräder
Fahrgestell	Zentralrohrrahmen mit hinterer Gabel und angeschweißter Plattform
Vorderachse	Einzelradaufhängung durch Längslenker; 2 lamellierte, querliegende, in Tragrohren geschützte Drehfederstäbe
Hinterachse	Einzelradaufhängung durch Pendel-Halbachsen mit Längslenkern; ein Drehfederstab auf jeder Seite, geschützt im Rahmenquerrohr eingebaut
Stoßdämpfer	Vorn und hinten doppeltwirkende hydraulische Teleskop-Stoßdämpfer
Bereifung	schlauchlose, großvolumige Superballonreifen, fünffach, 5,60-15
Fußbremse	Hydraulische Vierradbremse (Ate)

Radstand	2400 mm Wendekreis etwa 11 m
Spurweite	vorn 1290 mm, hinten 1250 mm
Abmessungen über alles	Länge 4070 mm Höhe 1500 mm Breite 1540 mm
Gewichte	Leergewicht 800 kg, Nutzlast 360 kg, zulässiges Gesamtgewicht 1160 kg
Kraftstoffbehälter	40 l, davon 5 l Reserve
Fahrleistungen	Kraftstoff-Normverbrauch 6,5 l/100 km, Kraftstoff-Durchschnittsverbrauch 7,5 l/100 km, Dauer- und Höchstgeschwindigkeit 110 km/h
Steigfähigkeit	1. Gang 34%, 2. Gang 17%, 3. Gang 10,5%, 4. Gang 5,5%

Laut VDA-Revers techn. Angaben entsprechend DIN 70020 und 70030

Sitze im bestgefederten Raum zwischen den Achsen. Kopf-, Bein- und Ellenbogenfreiheit für alle Insassen. Unter der Vorderhaube und hinter den Rücksitzen reichlich Platz für viel Gepäck. Motor im Heck, am gut zugänglichen, betriebsgünstigsten Platz. Großer Kraftstoff-Tank mit Reserve. Leicht schaltbares, gut abgestuftes Synchron-Getriebe. VW-Luftkühlung, bewährt in arktischen und tropischen Temperaturen.

VOLKSWAGENWERK GMBH · WOLFSBURG

Änderungen vorbehalten · Printed in Germany · Druck A. Bagel, Düsseldorf

Überreicht durch

RAFFAY & CO.
Volkswagenhaus
zwischen Jungfernstieg und Alstertor
Ballindamm 35
Ruf: 33 12 91   Ruf: · 44 11 71

---

of particular note—

thereby a true VW!

...lusive automobiles are commonly a technical gamble because ...eat test of series production is lacking. With the VW convertible ...isk does not exist. It is tastefully matured, and attracts many ...us glances. It is elevated to the realm of a precious thing by its ...pleasant and useful details. Here the driver has all the VW values ...ave made the Volkswagen famous and desired all over the world, ...d by millions of cars and constant further development.

...r:	Air-cooled 4-cylinder 4-stroke rear-mounted boxer motor, cylinder bore 77 mm, stroke 64 mm, displacement 1192cc, 30 hp at 3400 rpm, compression ratio 6.6 : 1, dropped valves.
...uretor:	Downdraft with accelerator pump.
...ng:	Air-cooled by blower fan, automatically regulated by thermostat.
...cation:	Pressure lubrication with oil cooler in fan's airstream.
...box:	2nd, 3rd and 4th gears synchronized. Transmission:
...sis:	Central-tube frame with rear fork and welded platform.
... axle:	Independent suspension by longitudinal links, 2 transverse laminated torsion bars in housing.
... axle:	Independent suspension by swing half-axles with longitudinal links, built into frame tubes.
...t absorbers:	Double-acting front and rear hydraulic telescopic.
... brakes:	Hydraulic four-wheel brakes (Ate).
...lbase:	2400 mm. Turning circle: approx. 36 feet.
...:	Front 1290 mm, rear 1250 mm.
...nsions:	Length: 13.35 feet. Width: 5 feet. Height: 5 feet overall.
...hts:	Dry weight 1760 lbs., load limit 792 lbs., allowable gross weight 2552 lbs.
...tank:	10.5 gallons, including 5-quart reserve.
...rmance:	Fuel consumption (steady speed) 7 quarts per 62 miles; average 2 gallons per 62 miles; cruising and top speed 68 mph.
...bing ability:	1st gear 34%, 2nd 17%, 3rd 10.5%, 4th 5.5%.

...ding to VDA data and German Industrial Norms.

...in well-sprung area between the axles, head-, leg- and elbow ...for all occupants. Under the front hood and behind the rear seats ...is ample space for luggage. Rear engine easily is accessible for ...e. Large fuel tank with reserve. Easily shifted, well-spaced ...ronized gears. VW air-cooling, proved in Arctic and tropic ...eratures.

VOLKSWAGEN WORKS INC. WOLFSBURG
(plus dealer's name and address)

With the convertible body by Karmann, the car naturally offered all the advantages of the workhorse VW Beetle.

Who would not feel a burning desire to drive such a car upon seeing pictures like these? Incidentally, the Volkswagen still had directional signal arms at that time.

Cars

VW SEDAN (standard model)
Standard paint
Primed
Extra price for sun roof (made by Golde)

VW SEDAN (export model)
Standard paint
Primed
Extra price for sun roof (made by Golde)

VW CONVERTIBLE four-seater, your choice of leatherette
combined fabric and leatherette upholstery, standard paint

VW KARMANN GHIA COUPE (on VW export model chassis), y
choice of leatherette or combined fabric and leatherette upholst
standard paint

VW KARMANN GHIA CONVERTIBLE (on VW export mo
chassis), your choice of leatherette or combined fabric-leather
upholstery, standard paint

Vans

VW COVERED VAN
Standard paint
Primed
Extra price for struts and canvas top

VW COVERED VAN with double cab
Standard paint
Primed
Extra price for struts and canvas top

VW LARGE-SIZE COVERED VAN
Standard paint
Primed

**FOR THE VALUABLE VW
VALUABLE VW SERVICE**

VW LARGE-SIZE WOOD VAN
Standard Paint
Primed

VW BOX VAN
Standard paint
Primed

VW BOX VAN with doors on both sides
Standard paint
Primed

VW KOMBI without seats in rear
Standard paint
Primed Extra price for sun roof (made by Golde)

VW KOMBI with seats for 7 or 8 persons counting driver
Standard paint
Primed
Extra price for sun roof (made by Golde)

VW 7-SEATER AND VW 8-SEATER with complete seating in
passenger area
Standard paint
Primed
Extra price for sun roof (made by Golde)

VW 7-SEATER AND 8-SEATER "SPECIAL MODEL" with com
seating in the passenger area, windows and perimeter window
around, and sun roof (made by Golde)
Standard paint
Primed

VW AMBULANCE with two stretchers and complete equip
Standard paint

When the Convertible Still Didn't Cost 6000 Marks

Price List

Purchasing a Volkswagen is made easier by the favorable conditions of the Volkswagen Financing Corporation (finance charge for 12 months only 6.8%).

A service plan designed to suit the VW driver (VVD) offers individual service and secure protection.

Every VW dealer gladly will provide information.

As of August 1, 1960

The right to make changes—including the finance charge—is reserved.

Prices f.o.b. the factory in Wolfsburg, Hannover or other factory.

Included in the price: one spare wheel with tire and a complete set of tools.

The interesting price list of VW automobiles of more than 25 years ago. The price of the standard model reached its lowest point of 3790 DM from 1957 to 1961. That was a lot of car for the money! The convertible cost 5990 DM.

Always a feast for the
eyes! Advertising
pictures from the
fifties, when drawings
still were preferred over
photos.

Leicht erfüllbare Sonderwünsche

Ganz nach persönlichem Geschmack nette und nützliche Details gegen entsprechenden Aufpreis

Page 33 text identical to upper part of page 27.

Spezial-Reiseeinsatz
wechselnd benutzbar als Sitzbank oder Großgepäck-Plateau (an Stelle der serienmäßigen Sitzbank)

Beleuchtete Zeituhr, rechts vom Zentralinstrument

Weißwand-Reifen, Hochglanz-Metallköder

Armkissen in Art und Farbe der Bezüge

Einknöpfbare Schutzhülle für Volant und Fond; gleichzeitig für Fond und Gepäckraum verschließbar

Whether in city traffic or on mountain roads, one met growing numbers of VW models everywhere; in America the numbers of **Beetle** fans also grew very quickly.

34 PS und vollsynchron

The Convertible
34 hp and fully synchronized

Whoever loves plenty of sun and fresh air during a trip and sets high standards for a car's fittings finds the VW CONVERTIBLE with all the advantages of the export sedan and a weathertight, airtight top that can be opened and closed easily in seconds. Timelessly beautiful in body form and lines, it also offers the maximum in driving comfort and travel enjoyment.

The buyer can choose among numerous carefully matched color combinations for every individual taste. Rich chrome and highly polished trim stress the noble style of the car. Durable highly polished metal corners protect the rear fenders. The interior fittings naturally include sun visors, footrests and a handhold in front of the passenger seat. The glove compartment can be locked. Closed—even with the windows open—the thickly padded, sound-absorbing folding top with the large rear window offers the same protection against dust, wind and weather as the steel roof of the sedan. Open, with fully lowering side pieces, this uncompromising full convertible with its sporty air is the right car for nature-loving motorists. But it is always a reliable, useful car for occupation and business—always a very representative automobile that also is appreciated by the lady at the wheel.

The VW convertible unites sensitive elegance and cleverly designed practicality, technical progress and economic sense in a remarkably good combination. Wherever beautiful cars move forward, the VW convertible finds unlimited recognition, admiration and many desiring glances.

Wer viel Sonne und Luft während der Fahrt liebt und dazu hohe Ansprüche an die Ausstattung stellt, findet im VW-CABRIOLET das elegante Automobil mit allen Vorzügen der Export-Limousine und einem wetterfesten, zugdichten Verdeck, das sich bequem in Sekunden öffnen und schließen läßt. Zeitlos schön in Karosserieform und -linie, bietet es zugleich ein Maximum an Fahrkomfort und Reisegenuß.

Der Käufer hat die Wahl zwischen mehreren sorgfältig aufeinander abgestimmten Farbkombinationen für jeden individuellen Geschmack. Reiche Chromverzierungen und hochglanzpolierte Schmuckleisten betonen den noblen Stil des Wagens. Widerstandsfähige Hochglanzmetallecken schützen die hinteren Kotflügel. Zur Innenausstattung gehören selbstverständlich Sonnenblende, Fußstütze und Haltegriff vor dem Beifahrersitz. Der Handschuhkasten ist verschließbar. Geschlossen —

auch bei geöffneten Fenstern — bietet das dickwattierte, geräuschverzehrende Faltverdeck mit dem auffallend großen Heckfenster die gleiche Geborgenheit, den gleichen Schutz gegen Staub, Wind und Wetter wie das Stahldach der Limousine. Offen, mit völlig versenkten Seitenteilen, ist dieses kompromißlose, sportlich wirkende Voll-Cabriolet der richtige Wagen für naturliebende Automobilisten. Immer aber ist es ein zuverlässiges Gebrauchsfahrzeug für Beruf und Geschäft — immer ein sehr repräsentatives Automobil, das deshalb auch von der Dame am Steuer besonders geschätzt wird.

So vereinigen sich im VW-Cabriolet sinnvolle Eleganz und klug durchdachte Zweckmäßigkeit, technischer Fortschritt und wirtschaftliche Vernunft zu einer erstaunlich guten Lösung. Wo immer schöne Wagen vorfahren: das VW-Cabriolet findet uneingeschränkte Anerkennung, Bewunderung und manchen begehrenden Blick.

In August 1960 the car received numerous important improvements, including an additional four horsepower, a fully synchronized gearbox, an automatic choke and an ignition-starter lock.

Technical

MOTOR

Construction:	4-cylinder 4-stroke carburetor motor	
	Crankshaft:	Four bearings
Cylinders:	Boxer motor, 2 opposed banks of 2 cylinders	
Valves:	Dropped	
	Cylinder bore:	77 mm; Stroke:
Displacement:	1192 cc	
Compression:	7.0 : 1 (export model and convertible), 6.6 : 1 (standard model)	
Horsepower:	34 hp at 3600 rpm (export model and convertible), 30 hp at 3400 rpm (standard model)	
Piston speed:	7.68 m/s at 3600 rpm (export model and convertible), 7.25 m/s at 3400 rpm (standard model)	
	Lubrication:	Pressure lubrica
Oil capacity:	2.5 quarts	
Fuel feed:	Mechanical fuel pump	
Carburetor:	Solex 28 PICT downdraft with automatic choke and accelerator pump (export model and convertible), Solex 28PCI downdraft with accelerator pump (standard model)	
Air cleaner:	Oil bath filter	
Cooling:	Air-cooling by blower, automatically controlled by thermostat	
Battery:	6-volt, 44 Ah	
Starter:	Pressure-screw drive	
Generator:	180-watt, tension-regulated	
Clutch:	Single-plate dry coupling	

GEARS

Export Model and Convertible:

Construction:	Four-speed gearbox, 1st, 2nd, 3rd and 4th gears synchronized
Ratios:	1st gear: 3.80, 2nd: 2.06, 3rd: 1.32, 4th: 0.89, reverse: 3.86

Standard Model:

Construction:	Four-speed gearbox, low-sound 3rd and 4th gears
Ratios:	1st gear: 3.60, 2nd: 2.07, 3rd: 1.25, 4th: 0.80, reverse: 6.60

AXLE DRIVE

Power transmission:	By spiral bevel wheel, transmission and swing axles to the rear wheels
Ratios:	4.375 (export model and convertible) 4.43 (standard model)
Oil capacity:	Gearbox and rear axle: 3.0 quarts (export model and convertible) 2.5 quarts (standard model) Filling amounts at oil change: 2.5 quarts (export model and convertible) 2.0 quarts (standard model)

Man fährt im Flachland wie im Gebirge, auf der Autobahn wie auf abseitigen Straßen, beruflich wie bei der Verwirklichung kühner Ferienpläne, immer sicher und gut im VW. Und man kann sorglos mit ihm reisen, nämlich im berechtigten Vertrauen auf das weitgespannte, engmaschige Netz von Kundendienst-Werkstätten, die überall und jederzeit zur flinken Wartung und fachmännischen Instandsetzung bereit sind. Als VW-Fahrer findet man rasch ein Zuhause für seinen Wagen — im deutschen Bundesgebiet allein bei gut 1300 VW-Spezial-Werkstätten; in der Schweiz verfügt man über mehr als 250, in Österreich über fast 200 Service-Stationen. Ähnlich ist es in den meisten europäischen Ländern und in Übersee. Insgesamt sind es mehr als 5000

VW-Werkstätten mit 43 000 Spezialkräften, auf die man sich in aller Welt verlassen kann. Werkgeschultes Fachpersonal, kontrollierte Werkstatt-Einrichtungen, sorgfältig kalkulierte Arbeitspreise, eine zentral gesteuerte Ersatzteile-Bereitstellung und ein seit Jahren bewährtes, gut eingespieltes Austausch-System für im Werk generalüberholte Aggregate machen diese einzigartige Kundendienst-Organisation zu einem Musterbeispiel der Zuverlässigkeit, Preiswürdigkeit und Zeitersparnis bei Wagenpflege, Reparaturen und der Erfüllung von Sonderwünschen. Damit entfallen für den VW-Käufer finanzielle Risiken, denen man sonst allzu häufig ausgesetzt ist; außerdem bleibt ihm bei solcher Wagenbetreuung der gute Wert seines VW viele Jahre lang erhalten.

One drives in the flatlands as in the mountains, on the Autobahn as on back roads, on business or to fulfill bold vacation plans, always safe and well in a VW. One cantravel carefree in it with justified confidence in the widespread, close-knit network of service agencies ready for quick service and expert repair work anywhere and anytime. As a VW driver, one quickly finds a home for one's car—there are approximately 1300 VW service agencies in the Federal Republic alone, 250 in Switzerland, almost 200 in Austria. It is similar in most European countries and overseas. In all there are more than 5000 VW agencies with 43,000 trained specialists on whom one can rely all over the world. Factory-trained specialists, tested workshop procedures, carefully calculated prices for work, a centrally directed spare-parts service and a proven exchange system for components overhauled at the factory make this unique customer service organization a model of reliability, economy and time-saving for all kinds of car service. The VW buyer thus avoids the financial risks to which one all too often is exposed; then too, with such car service the value of his VW is maintained for years.

1961

CHASSIS

Construction:	Central-tube frame with rear fork and welded platform
Front axle:	Independent suspension by longitudinal links above and below, 2 laminated torsion bars in housings; stabilizer (export model and convertible)
Rear axle:	Independent suspension by swing half-axles with longitudinal links; one torsion bar on each side built into housing
Shock absorbers:	Front and rear double-acting hydraulic telescopic
Steering:	Special spindle steering with divided rack, hydraulic damper (export model and convertible), 2.4 wheel turns from contact to contact
Turning circle:	36.1 feet (export model and convertible), 37.7 feet (standard model)
Tires:	Five tubeless super-balloon 5.60-15 tires
Wheels:	Disc wheels with deep-bed rims, 4 J x 15
Brakes:	Export model and convertible: hydraulic foot brake on 4 wheels, mechanical hand brake on the rear wheels; standard model: mechanical foot and hand brakes on all 4 wheels
Wheelbase:	2400 mm
Track:	Front 1305 mm (export model and convertible), 1290 mm (standard model) rear: 1288 mm
Fuel tank:	10.5 gallons, including 5-quart reserve

OVERALL DIMENSIONS

Length: 13.35 feet; width: 5 feet; height: 4.9 feet

WEIGHTS in lbs.

Sedan:	Convertible:
Dry weight: 1628	1760
Load: 836	792

Allowable gross weight: 2464 2552

PERFORMANCE

Fuel consumption: 2 gallons per 62 miles (export model and convertible), 2 gallons per 62 miles (standard model), per German Industrial Norms

Speed: Cruising and top speed 71 mph (export model and convertible), 68 mph (standard model)

Climbing ability

Gear	Export	Convertible	Standard
?	43.5%	39%	37%
2nd	22.5%	20.5%	20.5%
3rd	13.5%	12%	11%
4th	7.5%	6.5%	6%

*Consumption plus 10 percent with half load at steady three-fourths of top speed.

Technical data according to VDA and German Industrial Norms.

Additional details: Ignition-starter key lock with starter repeating; export model's muffler with two chromed tailpipes; chromed hubcaps and bumpers; interior light with door-contact switch; spare wheel, jack and tools under the front hood; specially fitted with whitewall tires at extra price.

The purchase of a Volkswagen is made easier through the favorable financial conditions of the VW Financing Corporation: interest at 12-month rate only 6%.

A thorough description of the technical data from an inclusive catalog of the sixties. The top speed hardly had been improved by the additional four horsepower, but the car clearly had increased in climbing power.

Technisches

MOTOR

Bauart	4-Zylinder-4-Takt-Vergasermotor
Kurbelwelle	vierfach gelagert
Zylinderanordnung	je 2 Zylinder gegenüberliegend — Boxermotor
Ventile	hängend
Zylinderbohrung	77 mm *Kolbenhub* 64 mm
Hubraum	1192 cm³
Verdichtung	7,0 (Export-Modell und Cabriolet) 6,6 (Standard-Modell)
Höchstleistung	34 PS bei 3600 U/min (Export-Modell und Cabriolet) 30 PS bei 3400 U/min (Standard-Modell)
Kolbengeschwindigkeit	7,68 m/s bei 3600 U/min (Export-Modell und Cabriolet) 7,25 m/s bei 3400 U/min (Standard-Modell)
Schmierung	Druckumlaufschmierung (Zahnradpumpe) mit Ölkühler
Ölinhalt	2,5 l
Kraftstoff-Förderung	mechanische Kraftstoffpumpe
Vergaser	Solex Fallstromvergaser 28 PICT mit Startautomatik und Beschleunigungspumpe (Export-Modell und Cabriolet) Fallstromvergaser mit Beschleunigungspumpe Solex 28 PCI (Standard-Modell)
Luftfilter	Ölbadfilter
Kühlung	Luftkühlung durch Gebläse, automatisch durch Thermostat geregelt
Batterie	6 V, 66 Ah
Anlasser	Schubschraubtrieb-Anlasser
Lichtmaschine	spannungsregelnd, Leistung 180 Watt
Kupplung	Einscheiben-Trockenkupplung

GETRIEBE

	Export-Modell und Cabriolet
Bauart	Vierganggetriebe. 1., 2., 3. und 4. Gang sperrsynchronisiert
Übersetzungen	1. Gang 3,80 3. Gang 1,32 / 2. Gang 2,06 4. Gang 0,89 / Rückwärtsgang 3,88
	Standard-Modell
Bauart	Vierganggetriebe. 3. und 4. Gang geräuscharm
Übersetzungen	1. Gang 3,60 3. Gang 1,25 / 2. Gang 2,07 4. Gang 0,80 / Rückwärtsgang 6,60

ACHS-ANTRIEB

Kraftübertragung	durch spiralverzahntes Kegelradgetriebe, Kegelradausgleichgetriebe und Pendelachsen auf die Hinterräder
Übersetzungen	4,375 (Export-Modell und Cabriolet) 4,43 (Standard-Modell)
Ölinhalt	von Getriebe und Hinterachse: 3,0 l (Export-Modell und Cabriolet) 2,5 l (Standard-Modell) Füllmenge bei Ölwechsel: 2,5 l (Export-Modell und Cabriolet) 2,0 l (Standard-Modell)

FAHRGESTELL

Bauweise	Zentralrohrrahmen mit hinterer Gabel und angeschweißter Plattform
Vorderachse	Einzelradaufhängung durch Längslenker oben und unten; 2 lamellierte, querliegende, in Tragrohren geschützte Drehfederstäbe; Stabilisator (Export-Modell und Cabriolet)
Hinterachse	Einzelradaufhängung durch Pendelachsen mit Längslenkern; ein Drehfederstab an jeder Seite, geschützt im Rahmenquerrohr eingebaut
Stoßdämpfer	vorn und hinten doppeltwirkende hydraulische Teleskopstoßdämpfer
Lenkung	Spezial-Spindel-Lenkung mit geteilter Spurstange, hydraulischer Lenkungsdämpfer (Export-Modell und Cabriolet), 2,4 Lenkradumdrehungen von Anschlag zu Anschlag
Wendekreis	11 m (Export-Modell und Cabriolet); 11,5 m (Standard-Modell)
Bereifung	schlauchlose Superballonreifen, fünffach, 5,60–15
Räder	Scheibenräder mit Tiefbettfelge 4 J × 15
Bremsen	*Export-Modell und Cabriolet* Fußbremse hydraulisch, auf 4 Räder wirkend; Handbremse mechanisch, auf die Hinterräder wirkend *Standard-Modell* Fuß- und Handbremse mechanisch, auf alle 4 Räder wirkend
Radstand	2400 mm
Spurweite	vorn 1305 mm (Export-Modell und Cabriolet) 1290 mm (Standard-Modell) hinten 1288 mm
Kraftstoffbehälter	40 l, davon 5 l Reserve

ABMESSUNGEN ÜBER ALLES

Länge: 4070 mm   Breite: 1540 mm
Höhe: 1500 mm

GEWICHT IN kg

	Limousine	Cabriolet
Leergewicht	740	800
Nutzlast	380	360
Zul. Gesamtgewicht	1120	1160

FAHRLEISTUNGEN

Kraftstoffverbrauch	nach DIN 70030 7,5 l/100 km*) (Export-Modell und Cabriolet) 7,3 l/100 km*) (Standard-Modell)
Geschwindigkeit	Dauer- und Höchstgeschwindigkeit 115 km/h (Export-Modell und Cabriolet) 110 km/h (Standard-Modell)

Steigfähigkeit	Export-Modell	Cabriolet	Stand.-Modell
1. Gang	43,5 %	39 %	37 %
2. Gang	22,5 %	20,5 %	20,5 %
3. Gang	13,5 %	12 %	11 %
4. Gang	7,5 %	6,5 %	6 %

*) Verbrauch zuzüglich 10 % bei halber Nutzlast bei gleichbleibend ¾ der Höchstgeschwindigkeit

* Laut VDA-Revers technische Angaben entsprechend DIN 70020 und DIN 70030

Weitere Einzelheiten Zünd-Anlaß-Schloß mit Anlaß-Wiederholsperre ● Beim Export-Modell Auspufftopf mit zwei verchromten Auspuffrohren; verchromte Radkappen und Stoßstangen; Innenleuchte mit Türkontaktschalter ● Reserverad, Wagenheber und Werkzeug unter der Vorderhaube ● Sonderausstattung mit Weißwandreifen gegen Aufpreis

Die Anschaffung eines Volkswagens wird durch die günstigen Finanzierungsbedingungen der VW-Finanzierungsgesellschaft erleichtert; Gebühr bei 12 Monatsraten nur 6 Prozent.

1962

The Car with Its Own Spirit

People who know automobiles stress comfort, particularly in driving in sporty open cars in fresh air and sunshine. They look for technical requirements in a car with its own spirit. For such gourmets constructors and coachbuilders have created an uncompromising full convertible, timelessly beautiful in line and form, with completely lowering side parts. This is a car for pampered motorists, but without overly high demands on the pocketbook. It stands out through superlative driving characteristics, is high in performance but low in initial price and thrifty to maintain. Its noble style is charmingly highlighted by the harmoniously matched color combinations. It is an "individualist," built by those who know how to for those who know and love cars. Wherever it goes it draws attention to itself. No wonder that this car also is highly appreciated by the "lady at the wheel." Solid elegance, well-planned practicality, technical progress and economic sense have united with the Karmann body to form a well-balanced unity in the representative VW convertible. Driver and passenger lean back comfortably in softly sprung upholstered seats. In front of the passenger seat, footrest and handhold provide for the necessary security in fast braking. The wide front seats also can be moved forward or back in transit and also be set higher or lower; the backs are adjustable to three different angles. One sits just as comfortably in the back of the car. The thickly padded top with the large rear window is robust, durable and opens quickly. When closed, it offers the same coziness as the sliding roof of the sedan; semi-automatically folded, it is covered smoothly by a cover with piped edging. Two spacious luggage areas, behind the rear seat and under the front hood, are ready for large luggage. The covers of these luggage compartments are held in an open position by springs. The finely regulated warm-air heating with defroster ducts to the windshield has two inlet vents for the front and rear foot areas. The heater also can be set, if one wishes, so that warm air only enters the rear seat area. Standard production also includes fast-acting windshield wipers and a pneumatic windshield washer system with push-button activation. The dashboard is laid out for easy viewing, with fuel gauge (including reserve indicator); chromed radio grid; and lockable, roomy glove compartment. Also included are interior lighting, large door pockets on both sides, two padded sun visors, rear-view mirror, directional signals that turn off automatically, and asymmetrical nonglare light and anchor plates for attachment of seat belts for four occupants.

During the sixties advertising became noticeably more factual, and attractive drawings were dispensed with more and more.

38

gestimmten Farbkombinationen reizvoll betont. Er ist ein „Individualist", von Könnern für Kenner und Liebhaber gebaut. Wo immer er vorfährt, zieht er anerkennende Blicke auf sich. Kein Wunder, das dieser Wagen auch von der „Dame am Steuer" sehr geschätzt wird. Solide Eleganz und wohldurchdachte Zweckmäßigkeit, technischer Fortschritt und wirtschaftliche Vernunft

haben sich im repräsentativen VW-C mit Karmann-Karosserie zu einer wo wogenen Lösung vereint. Fahrer und N lehnen behaglich in weich gefederten sitzen. Vor dem Beifahrersitz sorgen F und Haltegriff für die nötige Sicher plötzlichem Bremsen. Die breiten Vord können auch während der Fahrt belie

Der Wagen mit eigener Note

Es sind gewiß nicht die schlechtesten Kenner des Automobils, denen es auf sportliches Fahren im offenen Wagen, in Luft und Sonne ankommt, die neben technischen Ansprüchen auch auf den Komfort besonderen Wert legen und ein Auto mit eigener Note erstreben. Für solche Feinschmecker haben Konstrukteure und Karosseriebauer kompromißlos ein Voll-Cabriolet geschaffen, zeitlos schön in Linie und Form, mit völlig versenkbaren Seitenteilen - einen Wagen für verwöhnte Automobilisten, doch ohne überhöhte Ansprüche an die Brieftasche. Er zeichnet sich aus durch hervorragende Fahreigenschaften, ist hoch in der Leistung, aber niedrig im Anschaffungspreis und sparsam im Unterhalt. Sein nobler Stil wird durch die harmonisch aufeinander ab-

r hinten gerückt und zugleich höher
driger gestellt werden; die Lehnen sind
rschiedenen Neigungsstufen einstellbar.
bequem sitzt man im Fond des Wagens.
wattierte Verdeck mit dem großen Heck-
st robust, haltbar und schnell zu öffnen.
ssen bietet es die gleiche Geborgenheit,
Schiebedach der Limousine; halbautomatisch zusammengelegt, wird es von einer
paspelierten Hülle faltenlos umschlossen. Für das
große Reisegepäck stehen zwei geräumige
Kofferdepots zur Verfügung, nämlich hinter der
Rückbank und unter der Vorderhaube, deren
Deckel in geöffneter Stellung durch Federn
festgehalten wird. Die fein regulierbare Warmluftheizung mit Entfrosterdüsen an den Scheiben

hat je zwei Einlaßdüsen für den vorderen und
hinteren Fußraum und läßt sich bei Bedarf auch
so einstellen, daß Warmluft nur an der Fond-
bank einströmt. Zur serienmäßigen Ausstattung
gehören ferner schnellarbeitende Scheibenwischer, eine pneumatische Scheibenwaschanlage mit Druckknopfbetätigung, die übersichtlich
aufgegliederte Armaturentafel mit Kraftstoff-Uhr

(zur Reserveanzeige), mit verchromtem Radiogitter und verschließbarem, sehr geräumigem
Handschuhkasten, Innenbeleuchtung, große Türtaschen an beiden Seiten, zwei gepolsterte
Sonnenblenden, Rückblickspiegel, Blinker mit
automatischer Rückstellung, asymmetrisches Ab-
blendlicht und Grundplatten zur Befestigung von
Sicherheitsgurten für vier Fahrgäste.

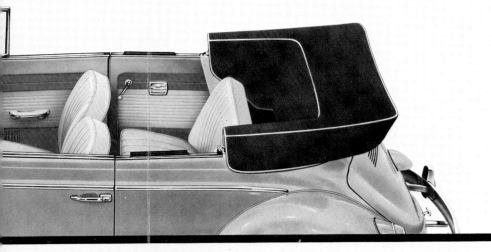

Technische Daten:

Vierzylinder-Viertakt-Boxermotor, Bohrung x Hub
77 x 64 mm, Hubraum 1192 ccm, 34 PS bei 3600
U/min, Verdichtung 7,0. Thermostatische Rege-
lung der Gebläsekühlung, Ölkühler im Gebläse-
luftstrom mit temperaturabhängiger Zuschaltung.
Zentralrohrrahmen mit angeschweißter Plattform.
Stabilisator an der Vorderachse. Leichtgängige
Schneckenrollenlenkung mit hydraulischem Lenkungsdämpfer und wartungsfreier Spurstange.
Kombiniertes Lenk-Zündanlaßschloß mit Anlaß-
wiederholsperre an der Lenksäule, mit dem bei
ausgeschalteter Zündung gleichzeitig die Lenkung verriegelt werden kann. Bereifung 5,60—15,
Radstand 2400 mm; Spurweite 1305/1288 mm;
Länge/Breite/Höhe 4070/1540/1500 mm; Kraft-
stoffbehälter 40 l; Reserveanzeige durch Kraft-
stoffuhr; Kraftstoffverbrauch nach DIN 70030:
7,5 l/100 km* Höchst = Dauergeschwindigkeit
1 0 km/h; Steigfähigkeit 1. Gang 39%; 2. Gang
20,5%; 3. Gang 12%; 4. Gang 6,5%.

*) Verbrauch bei halber Nutzlast und gleichbleibend ³/₄ der
Höchstgeschwindigkeit plus 10%.
Laut VDA-Revers technische Angaben entsprechend DIN 70020 und 70030

Technical data:

Four-cylinder four-stroke boxer motor, bore and stroke 77 x 64 mm,
displacement 1192 cc, 34 hp at 3600 rpm, 7.0 : 1 compression ratio,
thermostatic regulation of air-cooling, oil cooler in the airstream with
temperature-dependent control. Central-tube chassis with welded
platform, stabilizer on the front axle. Easily accessible worm-gear
steering with hydraulic damper and maintenance-free rack. Combined
steering-ignition lock with starter repeater on the steering column,
with which the steering can be locked when the ignition is turned off.
5.60-15 tires, 2400 mm wheelbase, front and rear track 1305/1288 mm,
length/width/height 13.35 feet/5 feet/5 feet; 10.4-gallon fuel tank,
reserve indication on fuel gauge, fuel consumption according to DIN:
2 gallons per 62 miles,• top/cruising speed 75 mph; climbing ability
in 1st gear: 39%, 2nd: 20.5%, 3rd: 12%, 4th: 6.5%.

• Consumption with half load at steady three-fourths of top speed
plus 10 percent.
Data according to VDA and German Industrial Norms.

Every year
improvements were
made: in 1961 there
were new rear lights in
two-section design; in
1962 new steering gear
and a fuel gauge to
replace the reserve valve
were added. A steering-
column lock made
things difficult for
thieves.

Like the Beetle in sedan form, the convertible was a lasting long-distance runner that one could drive on the Autobahn at full throttle for long stretches without a bad conscience. It was never too much for the motor.

Exklusiv, sportlich, ausdauernd

Kraftvoll im Start, ausdauernd auf der Autobahn, stark in den Bergen – das sind typische Eigenschaften des VW-Cabriolets. Eine technische Spitzenleistung ist der Vergaser mit Startautomatik; er gewährleistet schnelles Starten bei jeder Temperatur und geschmeidiges Fahren. Das günstig abgestufte, weich schaltbare Viergang-Vollsynchron-Getriebe und die spielend leichte Lenkung geben dem Wagen Gewandtheit auch im dichten Verkehrsgewühl. Lenkungsdämpfer, Stabilisator an der Vorderachse, Drehstabfederung, Teleskop-Stoßdämpfer sowie Einzelrad-Aufhängung machen das Fahren selbst auf weiter Strecke und angenehm selbst Genuß auf schlechten Straßen.Die starken hydraulischen Vierradbremsen fassen erstaunlich weich und

sprechen auf leichtesten Pedaldruck an. Auch individuelle Sonderwünsche sind erfüllbar. So können gegen Mehrpreis geliefert werden: ein Spezial-Reiseeinsatz,der die hintere Sitzbank zum Großgepäck-Plateau verwandelt, eine einknöpfbare Schutzhülle für Volant und Fond, Hochglanz-Metallköder, Weißwandreifen, Zeituhr und Armkissen.Automobile exklusiver Art sind oft ein technisches Wagnis, weil die große Serien-Erprobung fehlt. Beim VW-Cabriolet entfällt dieses Risiko; so geschmacklich erlesen es ist,so sehr es durch viele nützliche Ausstattungs-Details von sich reden macht: mit ihm verfügt der Fahrer ungeschmälert über alle VW-Werte, die den Volkswagen in millionenfacher Bewährung und stetiger Fortentwicklung berühmt und begehrt gemacht haben.

Exclusive, sporting, lasting

Strong at the start, steady on the Autobahn, strong in mountains—those are typical qualities of the VW convertible. outstanding technical achievement is the carburetor with automa choke; it assures fast starting at any temperature and smooth drivi The well-spaced, easy-shifting fully synchronized four-speed gearb and the playfully light steering give the car easy handling even heavy traffic. Steering dampers, front-axle stabilizer, torsion-suspension, telescopic shock absorbers as well as independe suspension make driving a pleasure on long trips and even pleasan rough roads. The strong hydraulic four-wheel brakes take he astonishingly lightly at the slightest touch of the pedal. Special ext also are available. At extra prices the following can be provided special travel inset that turns the rear seat into a large luggage surfa a snap-on protective cover from steering wheel to rear seat, hig polished metal accessories, whitewall tires, dashboard clock, a armrest cushions. Exclusvie automobiles often are often techni risks because they lack large-series production. This risk does not ex for the VW convertible. The car is appointed tastefully and attra attention through its many useful details. The convertible driver unlimited command over all VW values that have made the Vol wagen famous and desired through millionfoldproof and consta development.

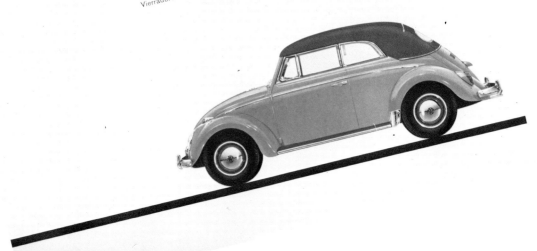

VW 1300 Cabriolet.

Es war immer schon eine schöne Sache, mit dem VW Cabriolet zu fahren. Ein so eleganter Wagen gefällt eben. (Auch den Leuten, die ihm nur nachsehen.)

Jetzt fährt man im sportlichen VW Cabriolet noch sportlicher. Der 40-PS-Motor gibt mehr Beschleunigung. Mehr Höchst- und Dauergeschwindigkeit. Und noch mehr Bergsteigfähigkeit.

Der Motor ist luftgekühlt, damit ihm die Luft nicht ausgeht.

Was diesen Wagen außerdem auszeichnet?

Erstens sein günstiger Preis. (Der niedrigste in Deutschland für ein Cabriolet dieser Klasse.)

Zweitens seine 4 Sitzplätze — das ist sehr selten für ein Cabriolet. Die meisten sind sogenannte 2/2-Sitzer.

Drittens sein Verdeck. Es ist doppelt: innen ein Dachhimmel, der die Querstreben völlig verdeckt. (Hell und freundlich in der Farbe, robust und haltbar im Gebrauch.) Außen ein starker Verdeckstoff, der wetterfest imprägniert ist. Dabei ist es leicht und schnell zu öffnen und zu schließen. Ein paar Handgriffe — und es liegt flach über dem Heck. Ein paar Handgriffe — und es schließt dicht.

Es ist eben ein VW Cabriolet. Sorgfältig verarbeitet auch im kleinsten Detail.

Übrigens ist auch die Heckscheibe im Verdeck — wie alle Fensterscheiben im VW — aus Sicherheitsglas. Sie verschrammt nicht und wird nicht gelb — ist also immer glasklar.

Die Seitenfenster sind voll versenkbar (alle vier). Das betont die schlanke Linie des offenen Wagens.

Die Innenausstattung ist die gleiche wie bei der VW 1300 Limousine. (Die gleichen bequemen Sitze. Den gleichen großzügigen Komfort. Selbst Kleiderhaken und Halteschlaufen hat dieses außergewöhnliche Cabriolet.)

Haben Sie Freude an Farben? An harmonischen Farbkombinationen? Mehrere verschiedene Möglichkeiten bietet Ihnen das Farbprogramm für die Außenfarben.

Die Tönung des Innenraumes, der Polsterbezüge und des Gummifußbodens sind darauf gut abgestimmt.

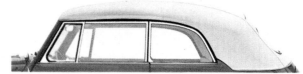

VW 1300 Convertible

It always has been nice to drive a VW convertible. Such an elegant car really is pleasing (also to the people who just watch it go by).

Now one can drive the VW convertible in more sporting style. The 40-hp motor provides more acceleration, more top and cruising speed, and even more mountain-climbing ability.

The motor is air-cooled so it doesn't run short of breath.

What else makes this car special? First, its reasonable price (the lowest in Germany for a convertible of this class). Second, its four seats—very rare in a convertible. Most are so-called 2+2-seaters. Third, its top. It is doubled; inside a ceiling that fully covers the struts. It is bright and friendly in color, robust and durable in use. Outside is a strong covering that has been waterproofed. It also is easy and quick to open and close. A few moves of the hand, and it lies flat over the rear. A few moves of the hand, and closes tightly.

It is simply a VW convertible; carefully prepared down to the slightest detail.

The rear window in the top—like all VW windows—is made of safety glass. It does not bend or turn yellow—it is always as clear as glass.

All side windows lower completely, emphasizing the slim lines of the open car.

The interior decor is the same as in the VW 1300 sedan. The same comfortable seats. The same great comfort. Even coathooks and holding straps are in this unusual convertible.

Do you like harmonious color combinations? The choice of exterior colors offers you several different possibilities.

The decor of the interior, the upholstery and the rubber floor coverings are nicely contrasted.

In 1965 the displacement was enlarged to 1330 cc, and at 40 horsepower the engine speed increased to 4000 rpm. The convertible now reached a genuine 75 mph and accelerated from zero to 62 mph in less that 30 seconds.

By the end of the sixties, the Beetle and the convertible achieved success throughout the world. There was scarcely a country to which VW models were not exported, and sales figures broke all records.

Warum ist der Volkswagen so beliebt in 136 Ländern?

Der Verkaufserfolg des Volkswagens ist einmalig. Wie kam es zu diesem Erfolg? Weil der Volkswagen, obwohl schnell und bequem, so wirtschaftlich ist, daß man ihn sich leisten kann. Weil der Volkswagen, obwohl heute auch andere Automobile einzelne seiner technischen Vorzüge aufweisen (den Heckmotor oder die Luftkühlung oder die Einzelrad-Torsionsstabfederung), so vernünftig all diese techni- schen Vorzüge in sich vereinigt, daß man ihn in 136 Ländern begeistert fährt.

In tropischer Hitze und arktischer Kälte. Auf modernen Schnellstraßen und Landstraßen letzter Ordnung. In den Bergen und auf ebenem Gelände. Weil der Volkswagen heute seiner Zeit voraus ist wie eh und je, weil eine gesunde Geschäftspolitik das Gute erfolgreich Jahr um Jahr verbessert. Den Volkswagen gibt es in fünf Modellen.
1) Als Volkswagen 1200 Limousine mit Export-Ausstattung. (Auf all diesen Seiten beschrieben.)
2) Als Volkswagen 1200 Limousine. (Etwas einfacher in Form und Ausstattung. Dafür aber noch billiger.)

Why is the Volkswagen so popular in 136 countries?
The sales success of the Volkswagen is unique. How did this success happen?
Because the Volkswagen, though fast and comfortable, is so economical that one can afford it. Because the Volkswagen, though today other cars show a few of its technical advantages (the rear engine, air-cooling or torsion-bar suspension), unites all these technical advances so sensibly that people in 136 countries like to drive it.
In tropic heat or Arctic cold. On modern superhighways or the worst roads. In the mountains and the flatlands. Because the Volkswagen is ahead of its time today as always, because a sound business policy successfully improves its good qualities year after year. There are five Volkswagen models.
1. As the Volkswagen 1200 sedan with export equipment (described on all these pages).
2) As the Volkswagen 1200 sedan (somewhat simpler in form and equipment; thus it costs even less).

1972

VW 1303 LS Convertible
For sporty driving in fresh air.

VW 1303 LS Cabriolet.

Für sportliches Fahren an frischer Luft.

In August 1972 the face of the VW Beetle changed for the last time. A big, arched windshield improved the view to the front, and under the rear hatch a 1600 cc motor now made a top speed of over 80 mph possible.

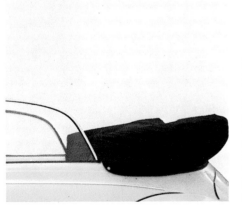

Left: As early as 1965 the convertible had been fitted with a new plastic top for ease of maintenance. From 1971 on the whole construction of the top became more compact; when folded it was about 5 cm lower and shorter.

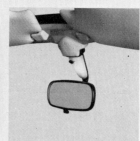

Right: The 1970 model already had standard front disc brakes. The dashboard was covered with black synthetic material and padded in 1972, and big round three-section taillights sat on the rear fenders from then onward.

With much safety inside and out.

In terms of safety, there is the large padded dashboard with handy switches gathered in one control panel, so you don't have to reach here and there. There is the new safety steering wheel with its big padded surface and element. There is the safety steering column and the dual-circuit braking system that still brakes if one circuit should fail (doubled holds better). There is the warning light for the dual-circuit braking system, which also serves as a warning for the hand brake. There are the safety door handles inside and out, a safety seat-back lock, and new three-point safety belts for the front seats (standard) as well as belt attachments for the rear seats.

There are the large taillights, so that you can be seen better. There is the VW automatic transmission (at a higher price), that makes driving even more comfortable and safe.

There are many other things that give you security, such as the nonglare safety inside mirror and manifold defroster system with blower.

Honestly, who would not like to own this classy car?

A convertible that is pleasing in line and form. The quality, technical perfection, long life and high resale value all in one—typical VW features that assure untroubled joy for many years. In winter as in summer, it always is ready to start. Built to high standards without being demanding. Robust, handy, economical: a car that unites the extravagance of a full convertible with the reliability and safety of the Volkswagen.

When will you take a test drive?

mit viel Sicherheit innen und außen.

Und dann die Sicherheit: Da ist zum Beispiel die übersichtliche, gepolsterte Armaturentafel. Mit griffgerechten Wippschaltern in einem Schalterbord zusammengefaßt, damit Sie nicht hin- und hergreifen müssen. Da ist das neue Sicherheitslenkrad mit großer Prallfläche und Prallelement. Da ist die Sicherheitslenksäule. Das Zweikreis-Bremssystem, das auch dann noch bremst, wenn ein Bremskreis ausfallen sollte. (Doppelt hält besser.) Da ist die Kontrolleuchte für das Zweikreis-Bremssystem, die gleichzeitig auch zur Kontrolle der Handbremse dient. Da sind die Sicherheitstürgriffe innen und außen, und die Sicherheitslehnenverriegelung. Und neu: Dreipunkt-Sicherheitsgurte

für die Vordersitze (serienmäßig) sowie Schraubanschlüsse für die hinteren Sitze.

Da sind die großen Heckleuchten, damit Sie noch besser gesehen werden. Da ist die VW-Automatic (gegen Mehrpreis), die das Fahren noch bequemer und sicherer macht.

Da sind noch viele andere Dinge, die Ihnen Sicherheit geben, wie zum Beispiel: Abblendbarer Sicherheitsinnenspiegel. Vielseitige Defrostungsanlage mit Gebläse.

Hand aufs Herz: wem gefiele es nicht, diesen schnittigen Wagen zu besitzen?

Ein Cabriolet, das gefällig in Linie und Form ist. Das Qualität, technische Vollendung, lange Lebensdauer und hohen Wiederverkaufswert verbindet — typische VW-Merkmale, die die unbeschwerte Freude für viele Jahre sichern. Im Winter wie im Sommer immer startbereit. Hohen Ansprüchen gewachsen, ohne anspruchsvoll zu sein. Robust, wendig, wirtschaftlich: ein Wagen, der die Extravaganz des Voll-Cabriolet mit der Zuverlässigkeit und Sicherheit des Volkswagens verbindet? Wann machen Sie eine Probefahrt?

With much comfort and high quality

Many other things contribute to comfort: the interior decor, clock, cigarette lighter, sun visors, handholds and the dashboard. You get all that in famous VW quality. Everything is made of fine material; everything is finely made. Service is based not only on factory-trained personnel but also on VW computer diagnosis. It makes service even faster and more reliable.

But you get a sense of speed and economy even sooner: when buying and when driving. First, there is no other four-seat convertible built in Germany at such a reasonable price. Second, the world-champion 50-hp motor makes the VW convertible 81-mph fast.

Its automatic choke makes it spring to life even in bitter cold.

The motor also is air-cooled, so it does not depend on cool water and anti-freeze. Its low turning speed guarantees a long lifetime. Its motor is satisfied with regular gas.

A powerful three-phase generator (50 A max.) and the prewarmed mixture of fuel and air make the cold motor even more flexible. We have nickel-plated the muffler so it will last even longer.

We have kept the great lines of the VW convertible.

But inside it a lot has happened in the last few years—a record for improvements.

Today the VW 1303 LS convertible has a sport-developed suspension that is built according to Porsche principles. There are transverse rear links and front coil springs. Every wheel is suspended independently, thus also independently sprung. That is why the VW convertible handles even rough roads without bucking and bouncing.

mit viel Komfort und hoher Qualität.

Zum Komfort gehören auch die vielen anderen Dinge: Die Innenausleidung, die Zeituhr, Zigarrenzünder, Sonnen-blenden, Haltegriffe und natürlich die Armaturentafel. Und all das bekommen Sie in der berühmten VW-Qualität. Alles also aus hervorragendem Material. Und in hervorragender Verarbeitung. Und mit einem Kundendienst, der nicht nur mit geschulten Fachkräften arbeitet, sondern auch mit der VW-Computer-Diagnose. Sie macht den Service noch schneller und noch zuverlässiger.

Schnelligkeit und Preiswürdigkeit bekommen Sie aber schon früher zu spüren: Beim Kauf und beim Fahren. Erstens gibt es im deutschen Automobil-bau kein anderes Viersitzer-Voll-Cabriolet zu einem so günstigen Preis. Zum andern macht der Weltmeister-Motor von 50 PS das VW-Cabriolet 130 Stundenkilometer schnell.

Seine Startautomatik läßt ihn auch bei starker Kälte anspringen. Der Motor ist außerdem luftgekühlt, so ist er unabhängig von Kühlwasser und Frostschutzmitteln. Seine niedrige Drehzahl garantiert eine lange Lebens-dauer. Seine Maschine ist mit Normal-benzin zufrieden. Ein kräftiger Drehstromgenerator (50 A max.) und die Kraftstoff- Luft-Gemisch-Vorwärmung macht den kalten Motor noch elastischer. Den Auspufftopf haben wir vernickelt, damit er noch länger hält.

Die große Linie des VW-Cabriolets haben wir beibehalten.   •

Aber in seinem Innern hat sich in den letzten Jahren viel getan. Ein Rekor[d] Verbesserungen.

Heute hat das VW 1303 LS Cabrio[let] ein sportlich aufwendiges Fahrwe[rk] nach dem Porscheprinzip gebaut Schräglenker hinten und Federbe[ine] vorn. Jedes Rad ist einzeln aufge[federt]. Also auch einzeln gefedert. Dan[n] das VW-Cabriolet auch schlecht[e] Straßen ohne Bocken und Sprin[gen]

As of August 1972 the VW 1303 LS convertible cost DM 8840. No other German auto manufacturer produced a convertible with four full seats for such a low price.

portlicher.

Wer schnell schaltet, sollte einen besonders griffigen Hebel haben. Und das Lenkrad immer fest in der Hand. Mit einem Drehzahlmesser kann man sportlicher fahren. Und den Motor schonen. Und wer seinen Käfer mit einem Steinschlag-

schutz ausrüstet, gibt ihm nicht nur eine sportlichere Nase. Sondern er sorgt auch dafür, daß sie auf schlechten Straßen nichts abbekommt.

13. **Schalthebelknopf,** aus Leder, mit Wolfsburger Wappen.
14. **Schalthebelknopf,** aus Edelholz, mit »VW im Kreis«.
15. **Schalthebelknopf,** aus Edelholz, mit Wolfsburger Wappen.

20. **Lenkradhülle,** mit Wickelschnur oder Druckknöpfen, in verschiedenen Farben.

23. **Rallye-Sitzbezug,** aus schwarzem Kunstleder, schalenförmig aufgepolstert, mit rotem Mittelstreifen. Für den linken oder den rechten Vordersitz.

26. **Drehzahlmesser,** Meßbereich bis 6.000 U/min, 85 mm Durchmesser, komplett mit Anschlußleitungen zum Einbau anstelle der Zeituhr in Typ 3-Fahrzeugen. In VW-Käfer-Modellen ist der Einbau in Verbindung mit der Instrumententafel mit Ablage möglich (siehe Position 25).

16. **Sportschalthebel,** verchromter Schaft, Knopf aus Edelholz.
17. **Sportschalthebel,** verchromter Schaft, mit schwarzem Kunststoffknopf.
18. **Sportschalthebel,** verchromter Schaft, Knopf aus Edelholz.

21. **Sportfelge,** aus Stahl, silbergrau-elektrotauchlackiert, Zierkappe aus Nirosta. 1 Stück.

24. **Sportsitz,** »Recaro-Ideal«, aus atmungs-aktivem Cordsamt-Material, mit Kopfstütze und Liegesitzbeschlag.

27. **Amperemeter,** Anzeigenbereich 30-0-30, Gehäuse-Durchmesser 40 mm.

19. **Sportlenkrad,** in Ledernarben-Effekt, 380 mm Durchmesser.

22. **Steinschlagschutz,** aus Kunstleder, für vordere Haube. Auch einfarbig silbergrau lieferbar.

25. **Instrumententafel mit Ablage,** mit genarbtem Schaumstoff überzogen. Vorbereitet für den Einbau verschiedener Instrumente, Schalter und Steckdosen.

28. **Fanfarenanlage,** verchromt, 1 Satz zum Außenanbau.

And even more sporting.

Whoever shifts fast should have a particularly graspable lever, and always have the steering wheel firmly in hand.

One can drive more sportingly with an rpm gauge and spare the motor.

Whoever equips his Beetle with a stone protector does not merely give it a sportier nose. He also makes sure nothing is chipped off it on rough roads.

13. **Shift lever knob** of leather with Wolfsburg arms.
14. **Shift lever knob** of hardwood with VW in circle.
15. **Shift lever knob** of hardwood with Wolfsburg arms.
20. **Steering wheel cover,** with cord wrapping or snaps, in various colors.
23. **Rally seat covers** of black leatherette, upholstered in cupped form, with red center lines. For the left or right front seat.
26. **RPM indicator,** calibrated up to 6000 rpm, 3.3-inch diameter, complete with connections to take the place of the clock in Type 3 vehicles. In VW Beetle models installation in connection with the instrument panel is possible with modifications.

16. **Sport shift lever,** chromed shaft, hardwood knob.
17. **Sport shift lever,** chromed shaft, with black plastic knob.
18. **Sport shift lever,** chromed shaft, hardwood knob.
21. **Sport wheels** of steel, electroplated silver-gray, with Nirosta hubcap, 1 piece.
24. **Sport seat,** "Recaro-Ideal," of breath-active cord-velvet material, with headrest and reclining control.
27. **Ampere meter,** indication from -30 through 0 to + 30. Case diameter 1.5 inches.

19. **Sport steering wheel,** in grained leather effect, 15 inches in diameter.
22. **Stone protector** of leatherette for front hood. Also available in plain silver gray.
25. **Instrument console** with receptacle, with grained foam covering. Prepared for installation of various instruments, switches and containers.
28. **Fanfare horns,** chromed, 1 set for external attachment.

The image of the convertible even could be improved with sporting accessories. Instead of flower vases, there were now three different sporting gearshifts—which did not make the car any faster but certainly looked impressive.

The Volkswagen Convertible. For all who like open driving.

The Volkswagen convertible is a car for individualists with special requirements, a car that sensibly combines comfort with power and durability.

For all who like sporty driving and fresh air, riding in this car becomes a special experience regardless of season or weather.

In rain, snow and cold the weatherproofed, five-layer top protects you.

In sunshine and blue skies, the top is loosened from its attachment and folded back with a few moves of the hand.

The seats are covered with durable leatherette and combine great comfort with sporting support—an important advantage on long trips.

The whole interior decor is tasteful. Everything is made of fine material and finely worked, in traditional Volkswagen quality.

The Volkswagen convertible gets power and endurance from its 37 kW (50 hp according to DIN) strong motor.

Its model roadholding is achieved with a sporting, highly developed suspension, with rear transverse links and front springs.

Safety steering wheel and column, a dual-circuit braking system with warning light, safety door handles and seat-back lock, and not least, the three-point safety belts for the front seats make this vehicle safe in the modern sense too. The Volkswagen convertible is able to meet high standards, robust and economical.

Das Volkswagen Cabrio

Das Volkswagen Cabriolet ist ein Wagen für Individualisten mit besonderen Ansprüchen. Ein Wagen, bei dem Komfort mit Kraft und Ausdauer sinnvoll kombiniert ist.

Für alle, die gern sportlich fahren und frische Luft lieben, wird das Reisen in diesem Fahrzeug zu einem besonderen Erlebnis. Unabhängig von Jahreszeit und Wetter.

Bei Regen, Schnee und Kälte schützt das wetter-

feste, fünf Schichten starke Verdeck.

Und bei Sonne und blauem Himmel ist paar Handgriffen das Verdeck aus der Ha gelöst und zurückgeklappt.

Die Sitze sind mit strapazierfähigem Kur bezogen und verbinden hohen Komfort mi licher Formgebung. Bei langen Touren ein v licher Vorteil.

Die gesamte Innenausstattung ist geschm

A Really Mature Automobile

alle, die gern offen fahren.

st aus hervorragendem Material und hervor-
d verarbeitet. In der bewährten Volkswagen
ät.

ft und Ausdauer erhält das Volkswagen Ca-
durch seinen 37 kW (50 PS nach DIN) starken

e vorbildliche Straßenlage wird durch ein
ches, aufwendiges Fahrwerk erreicht. Mit
glenkern hinten und Federbeinen vorne.

Sicherheitslenkrad und Sicherheitslenksäule, ein
Zweikreisbremssystem mit Kontroll-Leuchte, Sicherheitstürgriffe und Sicherheitslehnen-Verriegelung
und nicht zuletzt die Dreipunkt-Sicherheitsgurte für
die Vordersitze machen dieses Fahrzeug auch im
modernen Sinn sicher. Das Volkswagen Cabriolet
ist hohen Ansprüchen gewachsen, robust und wirtschaftlich.

The last version of the convertible was an extremely mature vehicle, thanks to its long production run. Every part had been improved, developed further or replaced by new aggregates in the course of more than 30 years of manufacture. The last model scarcely had a single part in common with the first. Only the characteristic shape of the car had been retained.

49

The Volkswagen Convertible. It looks even better closed.

1979

Because that's the best way to see the Volkswagen convertible top.

It overlaps the windshield frame, so wind, rain, and snow can't get in.

It's easy-to-clean vinyl on the outside. Leatherette inside.

In between are all the struts and crossbars (you never see them), and an inch-thick layer of horsehair and rubber insulation that seals out heat, cold, and noise.

The top is so thick you can't feel your hand through it.

And the fit is so airtight, it's easier to close the door if you open a window a little first.

The rear window is a real window. Safety glass. It won't split in the cold, yellow with age, or cloud up.

With all that goes into our top, you may be surprised how easily it folds out over the back. And back again.

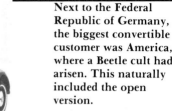

Next to the Federal Republic of Germany, the biggest convertible customer was America, where a Beetle cult had arisen. This naturally included the open version.

AUTHORIZED DEALER

Once again, Volkswagen promises you the sun, the moon and the stars.

1978 BEETLE CONVERTIBLE SPECIFICATIONS.

ENGINE:

Type	Air-cooled, rear mounted
Cylinders	4 cylinders, opposed
Displacement	96.66 cubic inches (1584 cc)
SAE Net HP	48 @ 4200 rpm
Fuel/Air Supply	AFC fuel injection

TRANSMISSION & DIFFERENTIAL:

Type	Fully synchronized, transaxle rear
No. Speeds	4 forward, 1 reverse
Final Drive	Rear wheel drive, double-jointed axles
Clutch	Single disc, dry

CHASSIS & SUSPENSION:

Frame	Semi-unitized body/chassis, platform with center tube
Front Suspension	Independent coil/shock absorber struts negative steering roll radius
Rear Suspension	Independent, torsion bars with trailing and diagonal arms
Service Brake	Dual circuit, drums front and rear
Parking Brake	Cable operated on rear wheels
Rim Size	4½J x 15
Tire Size	6.00 x 15
Steering	Rack and pinion

ELECTRICAL SYSTEM:

Rated Voltage	12 Volt, 50 Amp alternator
Battery	12 Volt, 45 Amp/hour

DIMENSIONS:

Wheelbase	94.5 inches
Length	164.8 inches
Width	62.4 inches
Height (Unloaded)	59.1 inches
Ground Clearance (Loaded)	5.9 inches
Turning Circle	29.5 feet (curb to curb)

PERFORMANCE:

Top Speed	80 mph
Fuel Consumption*	Highway: 30 mpg City: 21 mpg

*Based on 1978 EPA estimated mileage with manual transmission. Your actual mileage may vary, depending on where and how you drive, your car's condition and optional equipment. Ask your local dealer for a free copy of the EPA/FEA Gas Mileage Guide for New Car Buyers.

THE SUN, THE MOON AND THE STARS
ARE YOURS TO ENJOY.

CONTROL 5 FUNCTIONS
FROM THE STEERING COLUMN.

LUXURIOUSLY UPHOLSTERED,
SPACIOUS SEATING.

THE ONLY SMALL FOUR-PASSENGER
CONVERTIBLE IN PRODUCTION TODAY.

1979

One of the last VW convertible brochures from the USA before production finally ended on January 10, 1980. In all, 331,847 Type 15 convertibles were built—a world record!

The 1979 VW Beetle Convertible.

Treat yourself to one of life's little pleasures.

After 29 years, millions of Beetles, and countless improvements, the 1979 Convertible is still a very sensible way to flip your lid.

In fact, it's the only small four-passenger convertible in production today. And the only one that's built like a Beetle.

As you discover the sheer fun of owning and driving this sporty convertible, you'll also discover a dependable Bug underneath it all. With a bottom that's completely sealed with steel to keep out water, salt and dampness. And a body protected from the environment by three coats of paint.

The proven, 1.6 liter fuel injected engine delivers great performance. And according to E.P.A. estimates*, our Beetle Convertible delivers 30 mpg highway, 21 mpg city. So you can clip along with the sun on your face and fun in your heart, without getting clipped at the pump.

There's a top-quality top made of windproof, waterproof, easy-to-clean vinyl. And inside, it's fully insulated and upholstered to completely conceal the metal braces. The rear window, by the way, is a real window—glass embedded with electric heating elements to keep off snow and ice.

Go ahead. Raise the roof and let a little sunshine in.

1979 BEETLE CONVERTIBLE SPECIFICATIONS.

ENGINE:	Type	Air-cooled, rear mounted
	Cylinders	4 cylinders, opposed
	Displacement	96.66 cubic inches (1584 cc)
	SAE Net HP	48 @ 4200 rpm
	Fuel/Air Supply	AFC fuel injection
TRANSMISSION & DIFFERENTIAL:	Type	Fully synchronized transaxle, rear
	No. Speeds	4 forward, 1 reverse
	Final Drive	Rear wheel drive, double-jointed axles
	Clutch	Single disc, dry
CHASSIS & SUSPENSION:	Frame	Semi-unitized body/chassis, platform frame with center tube
	Front Suspension	Independent, coil/shock absorber struts, negative steering roll radius
	Rear Suspension	Independent, with trailing and diagonal arms, torsion bars
	Service Brake	Dual circuit, drums front and rear
	Parking Brake	Mechanical, operated on rear wheels
	Rim Size	4½ J x 15 Sports wheel
	Tire Size	165 SR 15 White wall, steel belted
	Steering	Rack and pinion
ELECTRICAL SYSTEM:	Rated Voltage	12 Volt, 50 Amp alternator
	Battery	12 Volt, 45 Amp/hour
DIMENSIONS:	Wheelbase	94.5 inches
	Length	164.8 inches
	Width	62.4 inches
	Height (Unloaded)	59.1 inches
	Ground Clearance (Loaded)	5.9 inches
	Turning Circle	29.5 feet (curb to curb)
PERFORMANCE:	Top Speed	80 mph
	Fuel Mileage*	Highway: 30 mpg City: 21 mpg

*Based on 1978 EPA estimated mileage with manual transmission. Your actual mileage may vary, depending on where and how you drive, your car's condition and optional equipment. 1979 EPA data not available at press time. Ask your local dealer for a free copy of the 1979 EPA/FEA Gas Mileage Guide for New Car Buyers.

AUTHORIZED DEALER

DAS KANN JA HEITER WERDEN...

...wir lassen die Sonne wieder rein in den Käfer.

Eine gelungene Idee, die im Grunde nicht neu ist. Sie steht auf bereits millionenfach bewährten „Rädern". Und damit diese auch wieder für Cabriolet-Fans laufen und laufen und laufen..., gibt es jetzt das ELLER CABRIO. Ein individuelles Konzept, sowohl „aufgeschlossen" als auch „zugeknöpft" unverwechselbar charmant. Das ELLER CABRIO macht immer eine gute Figur. Die Karosserie ist so verstärkt, daß es auch vollbesetzt mit vier Personen Haltung bewahrt. Durch den harmonisch der Frontscheibe angepaßten Überrollbügel bleibt das ELLER CABRIO immer in Form. Auch ein vorhandener Käfer kann zum Sonnen-Käfer umgebaut werden.

Heitere Aussichten für sonnige Fahrten.

THAT CAN BE JOLLY...
...we let the sun right into the Beetle.

A successful idea that basically is not new. It already has been proved a million times "on wheels." So they go on rolling and rolling for convertible fans, there is now the ELLER CABRIO.

An individual concept, whether "opened up" or "buttoned up," it is unmistakably charming. The ELLER CABRIO always cuts a fine figure. The bodywork is so strengthened that it still keeps its shape when filled with four people. With its roll bar harmoniously attached to the windshield frame, the ELLER CABRIO is always in form. An existing Beetle also can be rebuilt into a sun-Beetle.

Happy prospects for sunny trips.

The Last Convertible Did Not Come from Osnabrück....

Though the last open Beetle was shipped from Karmann in January 1980—there was still a convertible. The rebuilding of the sedan into an open four-seater (or even a two-seater, as Hebmüller had done) was undertaken by the Eller firm in Ober-Ramstadt. Unlike the original, this car had an almost completely stowable top. The handcrafted workmanship of this convertible was praised highly by experts. One also could obtain a light hardtop from Eller.

53

Die Basis ist millionenfach bewährt.

Wir bauen nicht irgendein Auto um. Nein, wir bauen den Käfer um – für Käfer-Freunde.

Seit Produktionsbeginn wurden davon bis heute mehr als 20 Millionen Fahrzeuge gebaut und dabei immer wieder technische Verbesserungen realisiert. Unser Cabrio steht also auf bewährten Beinen. Deshalb streichen Sie 1979 – damals wurde die Produktion des Käfer-Cabriolets eingestellt – am besten aus Ihrem Gedächtnis. Denn wir lassen die Luft wieder rein in den Käfer.

Eine luftige Sache.

Ein Cabrio nach Ihren Wünschen.

Sie können bei uns ein fabrikneues Fahrzeug fix und fertig umgebaut bestellen, in den vom VW-Werk jeweils lieferbaren Farben. Eines unserer weißen, schwarzen, sandfarbenen oder silbergrauen Verdecks paßt mit Sicherheit dazu. Ihren Gebrauchten bauen wir natürlich auch um – wenn er nicht älter als Bj. 78 ist. Und Ihren Ausstattungswünschen sind kaum Grenzen gesetzt: Unser Angebot reicht vom leistungsgesteigerten Motor bis zum aufsetzbaren Hardtop (in Vorbereitung). Also, das eller-cabrio.

Keine halbe Sache.

neue betriebsräume

Im seesengrund 18
☎ *06154 / 1551*
6105 ober-ramstadt

eller-cabrio

Eller · Spezialwerkstatt für Automobiltuning · Philipp Eller · Schuchardstraße 10
6107 Reinheim 1 · Tel. (06162) 5134
Stand: Oktober 1983 · Änderungen vorbehalten · Fotos: H.J. Kiersy (2), A. Krell (5)
Gestaltung: A. Krell · Druck: Lokay-Druck, 6107 Reinheim

Naturally, many mourned this classic car. The Eller firm tried to take advantage of this by rebuilding new or used VW Beetles (though none older than 1978) into convertibles.

WENN DAS WETTER KAPRIOLEN SCHLÄGT...

Vorwiegend heiter

Das Verdeck liegt gefaltet hinter der Rücksitzbank, versteckt unter einer chicen Persenning. So kommt die charakteristische elegante Form des Käfers voll zur Geltung. Und unter der Abdeckung bleibt noch genügend Platz für das Handgepäck.

Teils heiter – teils wolkig

Eine durchdachte leichte Konstruktion aus zwei Bügeln bringt das Verdeck in Form. Mit wenigen Handgriffen wird der mittlere Bügel eingesetzt und der hintere nach vorne geklappt. Jetzt wird das Verdeck an der Frontscheibe eingesetzt und seitlich befestigt.

Fortdauernde Gewitterneigung

Das ELLER CABRIO bietet guten Schutz. Das leichte Roadster-Verdeck ist aus erstklassigem Baumwollmaterial gefertigt. Der dreilagige Verdeckstoff ist in schwarz, dunkelblau oder dunkelbraun lieferbar. Und damit man nicht den Überblick verliert, sind Fenster aus hochtransparenter Folie eingenäht.

eller-cabrio

Eller · Spezialwerkstatt für Automobiltuning · Philipp Eller
Im Seesengrund 18 · 6105 Ober-Ramstadt · Telefon (0 61 54) 15 51
Stand: Juni 1984 · Änderungen vorbehalten · Fotos: F. Müller
Text und Gestaltung: B. Steeg · Druck: System-Druck Köln, 5000 Köln 41

The basis has been proved a million times.

We don't rebuild just any car. No, we rebuild the Beetle—for fans.

Since production began, more than twenty million vehic[...] been built, and technical improvements repeatedly have been a[...] Our convertible stands on dependable legs. So cross 1979—[...] production of the Beetle convertible ended—out of your mind[...] let the air back into the Beetle.

An airy matter.

A convertible as you like it.

You can order a factory-new vehicle rebuilt by us, in whateve[...] are available from the VW factory. One of our white, black, sa[...] silver gray tops will certainly go well with it. Naturally, w[...] rebuild your used car—if it isn't older than 1978. There are scar[...] limits to your wishes for equipment. Our offer extends f[...] enhanced-performance motor to a removable hardtop (in prepa[...] That's the eller-cabrio.

We don't do things by halves.

WHEN THE WEATHER TURNS CARTWHEELS...

Predominantly sunny

The top lies folded behind the rear seat, hidden under a ch[...] Thus the characteristically elegant form of the Beetle is fully[...] Under the cover there still is enough room for the luggage.

Partly sunny—partly cloudy

An ingenious light construction made of two bows brings[...] into shape. With a few moves of the hand, the middle bow is se[...] the rear one folded forward. Now the cover is attached[...] windshield frame and on the sides.

Lasting likelihood of rain

The ELLER CABRIO offers good protection. The light[...] top is made of first-class cotton material. The three-layer top[...] is available in black, dark blue or dark brown. So that one doe[...] one's view, windows of highly transparent foil are sewn in.

Karmann Ghia—A Charming Alternative

In close cooperation with the Carrozzeria Ghia firm of Turin, Karmann conceived a two-seater coupe as a sporting variant of the Beetle. In 1955 this new car was exhibited to the public. A convertible based on the Karmann Ghia followed two years later.

Italian Chic
and German Quality
All in One

Wie man das Karmann-Ghia-Cabriolet auch fährt – ob offen oder geschlossen: die Noblesse dieses Wagens bleibt untadelig. Ideal gelöst wurde das alte Problem des Karosseriebaus: wie ein Cabrio-Verdeck möglichst schnell geöffnet, zügig nach hinten gelegt und rasch wieder fest geschlossen werden kann. Zu dieser Lösung gehört vor allem der sinnreich konstruierte Zentral-Kurbelverschluß, der von beiden Sitzen aus bequem zu bedienen und im Handumdrehen entriegelt ist.

Das geschmeidige, spielend zu öffnende Verdeck fährt sich automatisch zusammen. Zur Hälfte versenkbar, liegt es trotz seiner guten, geräuschdichten Polsterung so flach im Fond, daß die sportliche Kontur des Wagens noch ausgeprägter zur Geltung kommt. Zugleich wurde ein sehr beträchtlicher Platzgewinn erzielt, der die für ein Cabriolet ungewöhnliche Größe des hinteren Kofferraums erklärt. Ebenso mühelos schnell kann das schützende Faltverdeck auch wieder wetterfest geschlossen werden.

However one drives the Karmann Ghia convertible—whether open or closed—the nobility of this car remains faultless. The old problem of building the body—how a convertible top can be opened as fast as possible, smoothly folded back and quickly closed firmly again—was solved ideally. The ingeniously constructed central crank attachment is a big part of the solution; it is reached easily from both seats and opened with a turn of the hand. The smooth, easily opened top folds up automatically. Half stowable, it lies so flat in the back, despite its good sound-absorbing padding, that the sporty style of the car is stressed even more strongly. At the same time a very large gain of space is achieved, which explains why the rear luggage space is so unusually big for a convertible. The protective folding top can be closed weathertight just as quickly and easily.

The central sections of the seat covers are made of nonfading, washable leatherette, always in pleasant color contrasts. Padding on the front edge, sides and back of the seat hold the body firmly in place. The door covers, made of two-tone synthetic material, are nonfading and washable, as is the perforated, "breathing" PVC canopy of the coupe. The convertible can, if desired, be delivered with seat covers completely of leatherette.

The Karmann Ghia convertible with opened visor! However you look at it—it is a masterpiece of technology and good taste. Admiring and desiring glances follow it. It is the lively, elegant car that one always dreamed of: modest price, high performance and of the best breeding.

Displayed at the 1957 Frankfurt Auto Show: the Karmann Ghia convertible on the Beetle 1200 export chassis. Equipped from the start with a transverse front stabilizer and directional lights. The coupe version appeared in the summer of 1955. The marriage of German technology and Italian styling produced a charming variant of the Volkswagen.

Die Mittelbahnen der Sesselbezüge bestehen aus hochwertigem Polsterstoff, die Seitenfassungen aus lichtechtem, abwaschbarem Kunstleder, immer in gefälliger Farbenharmonie. Schaumgummi-Auflagen an der Vorderkante der Sitze und seitliche Wülste an Sitzen und Lehnen geben dem Körper festen Halt. Auch die Türverkleidung aus zweifarbig abgesetztem Kunststoff ist lichtecht und abwaschbar, desgleichen der perforierte, "atmende" PVC-Himmel des Coupés. Das Cabriolet kann auf Wunsch mit Sesselgarnituren nur in Kunstleder geliefert werden.

Das Karmann-Ghia-Cabriolet mit offenem Visier! Wie man es auch betrachtet – ein Meisterstück der Technik und des guten Geschmacks, Bewundernde und begehrliche Blicke folgen ihm. Das ist der flotte, elegante Wagen, den man sich immer erträumt hat: preisgünstig, leistungsstark und von bester Rasse.

Eighty Mph
Was Not Fast Enough
for a Sports VW

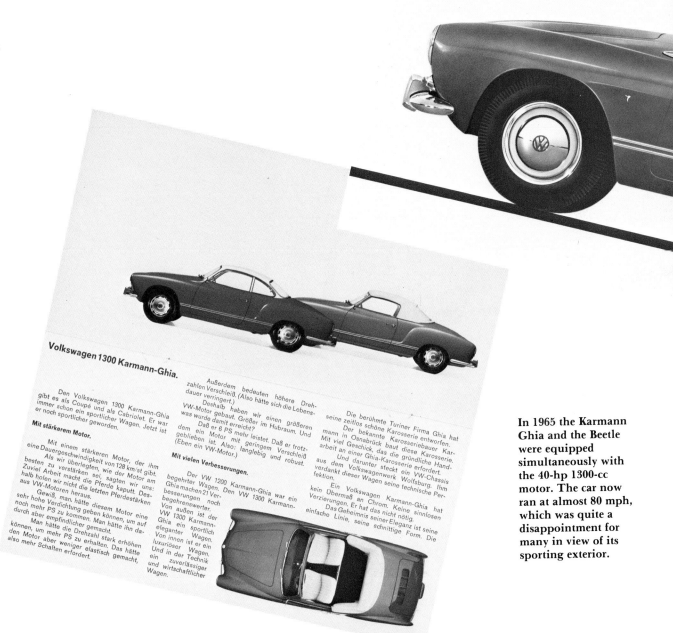

Volkswagen 1300 Karmann-Ghia

The Volkswagen 1300 Karmann-Ghia exists as a coupe and a convertible. It was always a sporting car. Now it has become even more sporting.

With a more powerful motor.

With a more powerful motor that gives it a cruising speed of 80 mph. When we considered how best to make the motor more powerful, we said to ourselves: Too much work ruins the horses. That's why we don't drain the last horsepower out of VW motors.

Of course we could have given this motor a very high compression to get more horsepower. But that would have made it more sensitive.

We could have increased the engine speed a lot to get more horsepower. But that would have made the motor less flexible and demanded more shifting.

Besides, higher engine speeds mean more friction. (That would have shortened its life.)

That is why we built a larger VW motor, with a larger stroke. THis provided 6 more horsepower. It is still a motor with little friction; thus long-lived and robust. (That's a VW motor.)

With many improvements.

The VW 1200 Karmann-Ghia was a desirable car. The VW 1300 Karmann-Ghia is made even more desirable by 21 improvements.

Outside the VW 1300 Karmann-Ghia is a sportily elegant car. Inside it is a luxurious as well as technically reliable and economical car.

The famous Turin firm of Ghia has designed its timelessly beautiful body. The renowned coachbuilding firm of Karmann in Osnabrück builds this body. The basic handwork on a Ghia body demands great skill.

Under it is a VW chassis from the Volkswagen factory in Wolfsburg, to which this car owes its technical perfection.

A Volkswagen Karmann-Ghia does not have a lot of chrome. or senseless decorations. It doesn't need them.

The secret of its elegance is its simple lines, its lively form. The...

Volkswagen 1300 Karmann-Ghia.

Den Volkswagen 1300 Karmann-Ghia gibt es als Coupé und als Cabriolet. Er war immer schon ein sportlicher Wagen. Jetzt ist er noch sportlicher geworden.

Mit stärkerem Motor.

Mit einem stärkeren Motor, der ihm eine Dauergeschwindigkeit von 128 km/st gibt. Als wir überlegten, wie der Motor am besten zu verstärken sei, sagten wir uns: Zuviel Arbeit macht die Pferde kaputt. Deshalb holen wir nicht die letzten Pferdestärken aus VW-Motoren heraus.

Gewiß, man hätte diesem Motor eine sehr hohe Verdichtung geben können, um auf noch mehr PS zu kommen. Man hätte ihn dadurch aber empfindlicher gemacht.

Man hätte die Drehzahl stark erhöhen können, um mehr PS zu erhalten. Das hätte den Motor aber weniger elastisch gemacht, also mehr Schalten erfordert.

Außerdem bedeuten höhere Drehzahlen Verschleiß. (Also hätte sich die Lebensdauer verringert.)

Deshalb haben wir einen größeren VW-Motor gebaut. Größer im Hubraum. Und was wurde damit erreicht? Daß er 6 PS mehr leistet. Daß er trotzdem ein Motor mit geringem Verschleiß geblieben ist. Also: langlebig und robust. (Eben ein VW-Motor.)

Mit vielen Verbesserungen.

Der VW 1300 Karmann-Ghia war ein begehrter Wagen. Den VW 1300 Karmann-Ghia machen 21 Verbesserungen noch begehrenswerter.

Von außen ist der VW 1300 Karmann-Ghia ein sportlich eleganter Wagen. Von innen ist er ein luxuriöser Wagen. Und in der Technik ein zuverlässiger und wirtschaftlicher Wagen.

Die berühmte Turiner Firma Ghia hat seine zeitlos schöne Karosserie entworfen. Der bekannte Karosseriebauer Karmann in Osnabrück baut diese Karosserie. Mit viel Geschick, das die gründliche Handarbeit an einer Ghia-Karosserie erfordert.

Und darunter steckt ein VW-Chassis aus dem Volkswagenwerk Wolfsburg. Ihm verdankt dieser Wagen seine technische Perfektion.

Ein Volkswagen Karmann-Ghia hat kein Übermaß an Chrom. Keine sinnlosen Verzierungen. Er hat das nicht nötig.

Das Geheimnis seiner Eleganz ist seine einfache Linie, seine schnittige Form. Die

In 1965 the Karmann Ghia and the Beetle were equipped simultaneously with the 40-hp 1300-cc motor. The car now ran at almost 80 mph, which was quite a disappointment for many in view of its sporting exterior.

Cabriolet

Mit em Karmann-Ghia-Cabriolet hat man einen wetterfest geschlossenen Wagen für unfreundliche Witterung und das rassige, offene Automobil für naturfrohes Fahren in Licht, Luft und Sonne. Ideal gelöst wurde das alte Problem des Karosseriebaus: ein Cabrioverdeck möglichst schnell öffnen, zügig nach hinten legen und rasch wieder fest schließen zu können. Zu dieser Lösung gehört vor allem der sinnreich konstruierte Zentral-Kurbelverschluß, der von beiden Sitzen aus bequem zu bedienen ist. Das geschmeidige, spielend zu öffnende Verdeck faltet sich automatisch zusammen. Zur Hälfte versenkbar, liegt es trotz seiner guten, geräuschdichten Polsterung so flach im Fond, daß die sportliche Noblesse des Wagens noch ausgeprägter zur Geltung kommt. Zugleich wurde ein sehr beträchtlicher Platzgewinn erzielt, der die für ein Cabriolet ungewöhnliche Größe des hinteren Kofferraumes erklärt. Mühelos schnell kann das schützende Faltverdeck auch wieder geschlossen werden. Die gewölbten Front- und Seitenscheiben gewähren vorzügliche Sicht; der Innenraum ist auch bei geschlossenem Verdeck auffallend hell. Da das aus elastischem Kunststoff bestehende Heckfenster bemerkenswert groß und zweckbestimmt weit heruntergezogen ist, besteht guter Ausblick auch nach rückwärts. Haubenzug und Handschuhkasten sind verschließbar; Vorderhaube und Motorhaube können wie beim Coupé von innen geöffnet werden. Weit umfassende, kräftige Stoßstangen schützen die VW-Karmann-Ghia-Modelle.

Convertible

With a Karmann-Ghia convertible one has a weathertight closed car for unfriendly weather and a thoroughbred open car for naturally happy driving in air and sunshine. The old problem of body construction—to open a convertible top as fast as possible, smoothly fold it back and quickly close it again—was solved ideally. For this solution the ingeniously constructed central crank attachment, that can be reached easily from both seats, is vitally important. The easily opening top folds up automatically. Half stowable, it lies so flat in back (despite its good sound-absorbing padding) that the sporting nobility of the car is highlighted even more. At the same time a very considerable amount of space was saved, which explains why the rear luggage space is so large for a convertible. The protective folding roof also can be closed quickly and easily. The bowed front and side windows afford an excellent view; the interior is remarkably light even when the top is closed. Since the rear window, made of elastic plastic, is noticeably big and purposefully extended far down, there also is a good view to the rear. The cover and glove compartment can be locked; the front hood and motor hood can be opened from inside, as in the coupe. Strong, far-reaching bumpers protect the VW Karmann-Ghia model.

At that time this type already had numerous improvements, such as larger headlights and wheel wells, emergency flashers, and a windshield-washer system; several minor items, such as an armrest on the driver's door (all as of the summer of 1959), were added to offer more comfort.

Manche mögen ihn als Cabriolet.

Alle Cabriolets sind romantisch. Daß ein romantisches Auto aber auch praktisch sein kann, beweist Ihnen das Karmann Ghia Cabriolet. Fangen wir beim Verdeck an. Vielleicht interessiert es Sie, daß zwei erfahrene Männer wenigstens vier Stunden brauchen, um es zu schneidern. Unsere Verdecke werden mit der Hand angepaßt. Mit der Hand gepolstert. Und mit der Hand vernäht. Was sie ziemlich von anderen Verdecken unterscheidet. Der Überzug ist aus PVC-Kunststoff. Die Mittelschicht aus einem Feinleinentuch und einer Gummi-haar-Matte. Und darunter ist ein Grobleinentuch und ein weißer Kunststoff-himmel. Durch dieses Dach kommt im Winter keine Kälte, kein Wind und keine Feuchtigkeit hindurch.

Und weil wir unsere Verdecke so sorgfältig bauen, daß sie genau passen, brauchen Sie sich auch über das Auf- und Zumachen keine Sorgen zu machen. Das geht ganz einfach.

Das Karmann Ghia Cabriolet kostet ein bißchen mehr als das Coupé. Aber das macht ihren Besitzern nichts aus. Weil sie wissen, daß sie für jeden Pfennig mehr auch mehr bekommen.

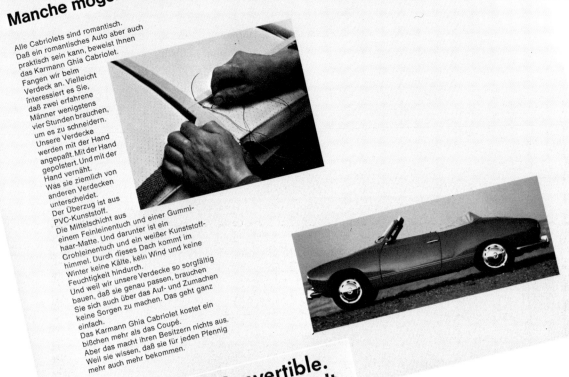

The Volkswagen Karmann Ghia Convertible. It looks even more like a sports car. It still isn't.

It's still a Volkswagen with a body designed by Ghia of Turin, put together by the Karmann custom coachbuilders.

Except now, a good part of that body is a top that's cut and fitted by hand, padded for insulation, and fitted snugly to the frame.

Whether the top is up or down, the Ghia looks more like an expensive touring car than a Volkswagen.

It is a touring car. It'll do 82 mph all day. But don't be misled. It'll also get about 28 miles to a gallon of regular gas. Average 40,000 miles to a set of tires. The engine is air-cooled, so it can never overheat or freeze. And it won't need tuning between tune-ups.

Does that sound like a sports car to you?

All convertibles are romantic. But that a romantic car also can be practical is proved by the Karmann Ghia convertible. Let's begin with the top. Perhaps it interests you that two experienced men need at least four hours to fit it. Our tops are fitted by hand, upholstered by hand, and stitched by hand. This differentiates them from other tops. The covering is made of PVC plastic. The middle layer consists of fine linen cloth and a rubber-hair mat. Under that is a coarse linen cloth and a white plastic canopy. No cold, wind or dampness come through this roof in the winter.

Because we build our tops so carefully that they fit perfectly, you need not worry about opening and closing. That works very simply.

The Karmann-Ghia convertible costs a little more than the coupe. But that does not matter to its owners, because they know that they get more for every penny.

For the pampered American market efforts were made to give the Karmann Ghia the image of a robust touring car with exclusive Italian design, since the underpowered convertible easily could be towed by any modest family sedan. The convertible top was as good as that of the open Beetle and made the car fully usable in winter.

In 1971 the Ghia types were equipped with box-section bumpers, and the dashboard was covered in black instead of the former wood-grain finish. In the engine compartment there was a plug through which "Computer Diagnosis" could be done.

Den VW Karmann Ghia wählen. Oben mit oder oben ohne.

Das feste Dach vom Coupé ist eine praktische und sichere Sache.

Aber für manche hat oben ohne eben seine besonderen Reize. Und schließlich ist das Verdeck des Cabrios auch besonders unkompliziert. Mit ein paar Handgriffen ist es zurückgeklappt und versenkt. Und mit ein paar weiteren ist es ruckzuck wieder geschlossen. Es ist so perfekt gefertigt, daß es auch bei strömendem Regen darunter trocken bleibt. Denn an diesem Verdeck

sind alle Nähte von Hand genäht. Außerdem besteht der Verdeckstoff aus fünf Schichten: einer aus wasserdichtem Kunststoff (ganz außen), einer aus Feinleintuch, einer aus Gummihaarmatte und einer aus Grobleintuch (in der Mitte). Und innen der eigentliche Dachhimmel ist aus abwaschbarem Kunststoff.

Jedes Verdeck wird auch von Hand eingepaßt. Damit's auch wirklich paßt.

Choose a VW Karmann Ghia. With top or topless.

The fixed roof of the coupe is a practical and sure thing.

But for many, toplessness has its own particular charms. Afte the top of the convertible also is very uncomplicated. With a motions of a hand, it is folded back and stowed. It is so perfectly that even in pouring rain it remains dry underneath, because a seams in this top are sewn by hand. Besides, the top material cons five layers: one of watertight plastic (outside), one of fine linen, c rubber-hair matting and one of coarse linen (in the middle). Insid actual canopy is made of washable plastic.

Every top also is installed by hand, so it really will fit.

by the way, "oben ohne" is really German for "topless", and I'r it was used deliberately. now on to page 63

12

Brand New: Computer Diagnosis

the VW Karmann Ghia. With reason.

example, there is its safety. The VW Karmann Ghia's dashboard upholstered especially softly on its forward edge. All control knobs cure. The safety steering wheel has a large striking plate and nt and is mounted on a safety steering column. The front disc s and the large-dimension rear drum brakes together have a lot of ng power. The independent dual-circuit braking system makes hat even if one braking circuit fails, the other one remains fully onal.

en there is its reliability. Its motor is robust. Its low engine speed ntees a long life. Its automatic choke always makes it spring to since the motor is air-cooled, it can never freeze and never eat. So that the Karmann Ghia remains as reliable as it is, you can ts heart and kidneys tested with the VW Computer Diagnosis.

VW Karmann Ghia always has had many pluses because of its my. The nickel-plated mufflers, for example, last longer. The ularly big tires last a few thousand miles longer than other tires. ng generator takes care of excellent energy supply. New disc s with thicker brake pads (and also longer life) are safer and can aired more easily if they need to be.

ides, what sports car is satisfied with regular gas?

Den VW Karmann Ghia fahren. Aus Vernunft.

Da ist zum Beispiel seine Sicherheit. Beim VW Karmann Ghia ist die Armaturentafel an der Vorderkante besonders weich gepolstert. Und alle Bedienungsknöpfe sind stoßsicher. Das Sicherheitslenkrad hat eine große Prallplatte und ein Prallelement und sitzt auf einer Sicherheitslenksäule. Die Scheibenbremsen vorn und die großdimensionierten Trommelbremsen hinten haben zusammen beruhigend viel Bremskraft.

Und das voneinander unabhängige Zweikreis-Bremssystem sorgt dafür, daß selbst bei Ausfall eines Bremskreises immer noch der andere voll funktionsfähig bleibt.

Dann ist da seine Zuverlässigkeit. Sein Motor ist robust. Seine niedrige Drehzahl garantiert eine lange Lebensdauer. Und seine Startautomatik läßt ihn immer anspringen. Weil der Motor außerdem luftgekühlt ist, kann er nie einfrieren

Und nie überkochen. Und damit der Karmann Ghia auch zuverlässig bleibt, wie er ist, können Sie ihn mit der VW-Computer-Diagnose auf Herz und Nieren prüfen lassen.

Zum Kapitel Vernunft gehört auch die Wirtschaftlichkeit. Hier hat der VW Karmann Ghia schon immer viele Pluspunkte gehabt. Die vernickelten Auspufftöpfe zum Beispiel halten länger. Die besonders großen Reifen halten ein paar

tausend Kilometer mehr aus als üblich. Ein starker Generator sorgt für ausgezeichnete Energieversorgung. Und neue Scheibenbremsen mit dickeren Bremsbelägen (also höherer Lebensdauer) sind sicherer und lassen sich, wenn es doch mal sein muß, leicht reparieren.

Und außerdem: welcher Sportwagen ist schon mit Normalbenzin zufrieden?

11

Volkswagen + VW 1500

Volkswagen Cabriolet 4-5 Sitze

Wer gern „Wange an Wange mit der Sonne" reist, ein leicht zu öffnendes und zu schließendes Voll-Cabriolet mit allen Vorzügen des Volkswagens wünscht, der wählt diesen Wagen. Geschlossen bietet das dickwattierte Verdeck den gleichen zuverlässigen Schutz gegen Wind und Witterung wie das Stahldach der Limousine. Ein Gebrauchsfahrzeug für Beruf und Geschäft, aber zugleich sportlich — richtig für naturliebende Automobilisten jeden Alters.

From a collectors' brochure of 1962 come the pictures on these pages. In 1962 the Karmann Ghia convertible cost DM 7635, a good 1400 more than the open Beetle, which gave it a certain exclusive character.

VW-Karmann-Ghia-Coupé-Cabriolet 2/2 Sitze

Hier zwei Wagen für den anspruchsvollen Kenner des rassigen, sportlich betonten Automobils. Keine teueren Luxuserzeugnisse! Auch diese beiden Modelle bringen alle Eigenschaften mit, die Volkswagen-Chassis und -Motor garantieren: also Wirtschaftlichkeit, Zuverlässigkeit, Dauerhaftigkeit. Beide Modelle werden wegen ihres chics besonders auch von Damen geschätzt. Im übrigen bietet in diesen Zweisitzern eine Hinterbank auch für gelegentliche Fahrten zu dritt oder viert Platz. Der große Kofferraum hinter der Bank wird doppelt so groß, wenn man die Rückenlehne nach vorn klappt. Ein zweites geräumiges Kofferdepot liegt unter der Vorderhaube.

Volkswagen + VW 1500
Volkswagen Cabriolet 4-5 seater

Whoever likes to travel "cheek to cheek with the sun," and wants an easily opening and closing full convertible with all the advantages of the Volkswagen, will choose this car.

Closed, the thickly padded top offers the same reliable protection against wind and weather as the steel roof of the sedan. A useful vehicle for business, but sporty at the same time; right for nature-loving motorists of all ages.

VW Karmann-Ghia Coupe-Convertible 2/2 seater

Here are two cars for the discriminating connoisseur of thorough-bred, sport-spirited automobiles. these are not expensive luxury products! These two models also include all the qualities that Volkswagen chassis and motors guarantee: economy, reliability, and durability. Both models especially are admired by ladies because of their chic style. In these two-seaters there also is a rear seat for occasional rides with three or four aboard. The large luggage space behind the seat becomes twice as big when one folds the seat back down. A second roomy luggage area lies under the front hood.

VW Convertibles That Could Never Be Bought

These two pictures are real rarities, for they show and offer two VW models that never actually were available. The new 1500 convertible designed by Ghia never went into production, and the open 1500 by Karmann also remained one of a kind, although a brochure was printed for it before the project was dropped.

VW 1500 Karmann-Ghia-Coupé und -Cabriolet

Seit jeher ist das Coupé oder das Cabriolet Ausdruck eines besonderen Lebensstils. Die individuelle Gestaltung beider Aufbauten — außerhalb der Massenfertigung — unterstreicht die persönliche Note der Besitzer. So auch bei den Karmann-Ghia-Modellen des VW 1500. Ihre formvollendeten Linien betonen den dezenten Charakter dieser Wagen, während die konstruktive Basis — Motor und Fahrwerk — in allem den übrigen VW 1500-Typen gleicht. Wer betonte Eleganz mit den praktischen Vorzügen des festen Aufbaues verbinden will, wird das Coupé bevorzugen. Dem mehr sportlich eingestellten Automobilisten steht dagegen das ebenfalls 2/2-sitzige Cabriolet zur Verfügung. Coupé-Ausführung auch mit Sonnendach (Stahl-Schiebedach) gegen Mehrpreis lieferbar.

VW 1500 Karmann-Ghia Coupe and Convertible

The coupe or the convertible always has been an expression of a particular lifestyle. The individual formation of both types—outside of mass production—stresses the personal note of the owner. So it also is with the Karmann-Ghia models of the Volkswagen 1500. Their perfect lines stress the decent character of this car, while the constructive basis—motor and suspension—are identical to those of all other VW 1500 types.

Whoever wants to unite striking elegance with the practical advantages of the solid body will prefer the coupe. For the more sportingly inclined motorist, on the other hand, the 2/2-seat convertible is available. The coupe style also is available with sunroof (sliding steel panel) for a higher price.

VW 1500 Convertible 4-5 seater

The sporting style, linked with the enjoyment of fresh air and sunshine, is a trend of our times. The VW 1500 convertible allows one to follow it in spite of the weather. In possession of all the technical advantages of the sedan, it also unites the long-lined elegance of the open car with the absolute weather protection of the closed body. The large bowed windshield is unusual in a convertible. Practicality and solidarity are united with beauty. The VW is an exclusive car that raises its owner above the auto-driving crowd everywhere.

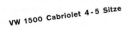

VW 1500 Cabriolet 4-5 Sitze

Die sportliche Note, verbunden mit dem Genuß von Luft und Sonne ist ein Zug unserer Zeit. Ihm je nach Witterung zu folgen, erlaubt auch dem anspruchsvollen Automobilisten die Cabriolet-Ausführung des VW 1500. Im Besitz aller technischen Vorzüge der Limousine verbindet sie außerdem die langgestreckte Eleganz des offenen Wagens mit dem absoluten Wetterschutz des geschlossenen Aufbaues. Ungewöhnlich bei einem Cabriolet die große gewölbte Rückscheibe. Zweckmäßigkeit, Solidität mit Schönheit vereint. Ein schon vom Äußeren her exklusiver Wagen, der seinen Besitzer überall aus der autofahrenden Menge hervorhebt.

Open Volkswagens with Special Bodies

Several coachbuilders, the firms of Drews, Dannenhauer and Stauss, Rometsch, Enzmann and Denzel, for example, turned the more or less down-to-earth Volkswagen into a racy roadster. A small selection of catalogs that illustrate these vehicles are shown to you on the next pages.

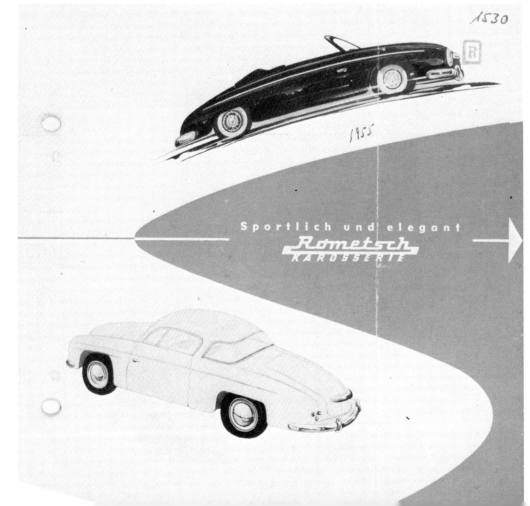

Sporting and elegant

Rometsch
BODYWORK

Probably the best-known special body for the VW chassis came from the Berlin firm of Rometsch, which transformed the VW into this streamlined sports car from 1951 to 1954.

Grand premier prix
Internationale
Schönheitskonkurrenz
in Genf 1954 und 1955

nd first prize
rnational beauty contest
eneva 1954 and 1955

ROMETSCH Special
rt Coupe and Convertible
he VW Export Chassis

tremely roomy despite the lowest body style. It offers three people
their luggage a comfortable ride even on longer trips. Wide doors
w easy entrance and exit.

he tasteful and readily visible dashboard and the elegant,
nonious interior decor,—comfortable, individually adjustable
seats as well as built-in warm-air heater and defroster make
g in a Rometsch a pleasure at any time of the year. While the top
e convertible is fully stowable, the rounded windows of the coupe
a good view in all directions.

Das ROMETSCH-Spezial-
Sport-Coupé und Cabriolet
für das VW-Export-Fahrgestell

ist trotz niedrigster Bauweise äußerst
geräumig; es bietet 3 Personen mit
entsprechendem Gepäck auch bei
längeren Fahrten ein bequemes
Reisen. Breite Türen gestatten ein
müheloses Ein- und Aussteigen.

Das geschmackvolle und übersicht-
lich angeordnete Armaturenbrett
und die elegante, harmonische
Innenausstattung, — bequeme, ein-
zeln verstellbare Vordersitze sowie
eingebaute Warmluftheizung und
Entfroster machen die Fahrt im
ROMETSCH bei jeder Jahreszeit zur
Freude. Während das Verdeck des
Cabriolets völlig versenkbar ist,
gestattet die Rundverglasung des
Coupés gute Sicht nach allen Seiten.

This Car Was Popularly
Known as the "Banana"

What the Berlin coachbuilding firm of Rometsch
made of the Beetle that suddenly didn't look like a
beetle any more. Rometsch also transformed other
manufacturers' sedans limousines into convertibles
and had an excellent reputation.

fortable—individual—economical—elegant

y ROMETSCH Model

hes the eye with its special styling. Available as a convertible or
e, it unites the good riding qualities of the popular, economical
sturdy VW chassis with an extremely elegant special body in any
ed color combination and luxurious interior decor. Despite the
solid quality work on the body, through the extensive use of light
l in the non-load-bearing areas, the total weight has been kept
arkably low. The aerodynamically favorable form gives the car a
top speed, and the outstanding roadholding provides a
fortable and safe ride thereby.

n honors at the meeting of
naster coachbuilders of
pe and America,
Remo 1954

The "Special Sport
Cabriolet" was
naturally more
desirable than the
coupe version that also
was available. This
car's interior space also
was reorganized
completely. Whoever
took a seat behind the
three-spoked ivory-
colored steering wheel
scarcely got the
impression of sitting in
a Volkswagen.

Komfortabel · individuell · wirtschaftlich · elegant

Jedes ROMETSCH-Modell

besticht durch seine besondere Linienführung. Als Cabriolet und
als Coupé lieferbar, vereinigt es die guten Fahreigenschaften
des beliebten, wirtschaftlichen und strapazierfähigen VW-Fahr-
gestells mit einer äußerst eleganten Spezialkarosserie in jeder
gewünschten Farbkombination und luxuriöser Innenausstattung.
Trotz solidester Qualitätsarbeit der Karosserie wurde durch
weitgehende Verwendung von Leichtmetall in den nichttragenden
Teilen das Gesamtgewicht außerordentlich niedrig gehalten.
Die aerodynamisch günstige Form verleiht dem Wagen eine
hohe Spitzengeschwindigkeit, und die hervorragende Straßenlage gewährleistet dabei ein komfortables und sicheres Fahren.

Hohe Auszeichnung
beim Treffen der
Meisterkarossiers von
Europa und Amerika.
San Remo 1954

This Rometsch model was a further development that was offered from the mid-fifties to the end of the decade. In comparison to the Beetle it had a very luxurious interior, and the sporty body with the stylishly curved panoramic windshield gave the car the American look that then was so popular then.

Rometsch
BODYWORK
BERLIN-HALENSEE
Founded 1924

SPECIAL BODIES
RECOGNIZED WITH NATIVE AND FOREIGN GOLD MEDALS

OUR STAR; SPECIAL SPORT CONVERTIBLE AND COUPE FOR THE VW EXPORT CHASSIS

THE BEAUTIFUL AND INTERNATIONALLY RECOGNIZED SPORT CONVERTIBLE AND COUPE FOR THE VW EXPORT CHASSIS

Eye-catching with its especially successful design and equipment.

Despite the simplest construction, it is extremely comfortable and roomy.

Favorable gross weight and center-of-gravity location provide increased top speed and outstanding roadholding.

Place for large suitcases in two luggage areas.

TECHNICAL DATA
Length: 13.45 feet
Width: 5.25 feet
Height: 4.4 feet
Weight: approx. 1804 lbs.
Chassis: VW Export

Already awarded the golden rose of Geneva in May 1957
A car for pampered taste
A car as elegant inside as outside
A car that gives its owner pleasure

Masterful Styling That Completely Disguised the Volkswagen

The Rometsch firm's last attempt was this convertible presented in 1961, with pleasantly strict styling. Despite "gold medals at home and abroad," it no longer found a market.

ROMETSCH
SPEZIALKAROSSERIEN

DAS SPORT-CABRIOLET

Modell 1961

Ein Wagen für den verwöhntesten Anspruch

SPEZIAL-SPORT-CABRIOLET UND COUPÉ FÜR DAS VW-EXPORT FAHRGESTELL

AUSGEZEICHNET MIT IN- UND AUSLÄNDISCHEN GOLDMEDAILLEN

Ein Wagen der jedem Besitzer Freude bereitet

TECHNISCHE DATEN	
Länge	4100 mm
Breite	1600 mm
Höhe	1350 mm
Gewicht	820 kg
Fahrgestell	VW-Export

Bestechend durch seine besonders gelungene Linienführung und Ausstattung.

Trotz niedrigster Bauweise äußerst bequem und geräumig.

Durch günstiges Gesamtgewicht und Schwerpunktverlagerung erhöhte Spitzengeschwindigkeit und hervorragende Straßenlage. Platz für großes Gepäck in zwei Kofferräumen.

ROMETSCH
SPECIAL BODIES

THE SPORT CONVERTIBLE Model 1961
A car for pampered taste

SPECIAL SPORT CONVERTIBLE AND COUPE FOR THE VW EXPORT CHASSIS

RECOGNIZED WITH NATIVE AND FOREIGN GOLD MEDALS
A car that gives its owner pleasure

TECHNICAL DATA
Length: 13.45 feet
Width: 5.25 feet
Height: 4.4 feet
Weight: 1804 lbs.
Chassis: VW Export

Eye-catching with its particularly successful design and equipment.

Despite the simplest design, it is extremely comfortable and roomy.

Favorable gross weight and center-of-gravity location provide increased top speed and outstanding roadholding. Room for large suitcases in two luggage areas.

UND COUPÉ FÜR DAS VW-EXPORT-FAHRGESTELL

TECHNISCHE DATEN	
Länge	4100 mm
Breite	1600 mm
Höhe	1350 mm
Gewicht	ca 820 kg
Fahrgestell	VW-Export

Bereits im Mai 1957 mit der Goldenen Rose von Genf ausgezeichnet

Ein Wagen der jedem Besitzer Freude bereitet

MCA Jetstar
Sports Car from a Master's Hand
THE CORRECTLY PROPORTIONED SPORTS CAR

From the connoisseur's viewpoint:
There is not much to say here—whether you take the rear engine with its excellent acceleration or the bucket seats of correct size with the ideal sitting position and the fine view to all sides...

FOR THE CHIC MOTORIST

DER MASSGERECHTE SPORTWAGEN

Von der Kennersicht:

Hier ist nicht viel zu sagen — ob Sie den Heckmotor

nehmen mit seiner ausgezeichneten

Beschleunigung oder die maßgerechten

Schalensitze mit der vollkommenen

Sitzposition und der hervorragenden

Übersicht nach allen Seiten . . .

FÜR DEN SCH

A Volkswagen That Hardly Anyone Still Remembers

The MCA Jetstar, constructed by Ulrich Otten in Bremen, ranks among the forgotten automobiles today, although several hundred examples are said to have been built. The streamlined synthetic body was mounted on a slightly widened Beetle chassis, and a 35 or 45 horsepower VW motor provided for speedy travel. The Jetstar was built at the beginning of the sixties.

...whether you test the warp-free chassis frame, the suspension and the wheel sizes—or perceive the beautifully formed synthetic body—whether you observe the length, width and height of the car, you will always come to the same conclusion: ◂

The correctly proportioned sports car by a master's hand

TECHNICAL DATA

Motor:	Four-cylinder four-stroke boxer motor in the rear, displacement 1198 cc, compression 6.9 : 1, performance 45 DIN hp at 4250 rpm, air-cooled
Electric:	6-volt 66 Ah battery
Power transmission:	Rear drive with differential, gearbox ahead of the rear axle, bevel-wheel drive (spiral-geared) 4-speed gearbox, 2nd, 3rd and 4th gears synchronized and 1st gear low-sound, stick shift
Suspension:	Rectangular tube frame with tube braces, independent front suspension with torsion-bar springing and telescopic shock absorbers, rear pendulum axles with longitudinal links, coil springs with shock absorbers inside.
Tires:	5.60 x 15 sport
Brakes:	Hydraulic foot brakes on 4 wheels. Mechanical hand brake on the rear wheels. 620 square cm braking surface
Body:	Fiberglass-reinforced polyester body with two doors. All-weather top and snap-on panels for the doors. Body welded to the chassis.
Equipment:	Leatherette-covered bucket seats. Speedometer with trip indicator (up to 125 mph). RPM indicator, clock, gas gauge, oil temperature gauge, cigarette lighter, ashtray, interior and exterior mirrors, warning lights, warm-air heating, wheels with crossed spokes.
Weights and Measures:	Length 12.8 feet, width 5.1 feet, height 3.8 feet, wheelbase 2130 mm, front track 1305 mm, rear track 1315 mm, ground clearance 170 mm, dry weight 2090 lbs., allowable gross weight 2090 lbs.
Speed:	93-100 mph, acceleration from 0 to 62 mph in 12 seconds
Consumption:	9.5 to 11 quarts, depending on type of driving
Tank capacity:	11.25 gallons
Special equipment:	Installation of special supercharger and stronger crankshaft, giving 55 DIN hp performance. Windshield washer system, safety lock, safety-glass windshield
Colors:	Florida yellow, purple-red, snow white, Riviera blue, pastel green

Constant further developments and improvements are a principle of the M.C.A. Automobile Factory. Therefore the right to make changes in construction and equipment as opposed to what is listed here is reserved.

You will be well advised...and a test drive is offered by (name and address of agency)

TECHNISCHE DATEN

Motor: Vierzylinder-Viertakt-Boxermotor im Heck, Hubraum 1198 ccm, Verdichtung 6,9:1, Leistung 45 DIN PS bei 4250 Upm, Luftkühlung

Elektr. Anlage: 6 Volt, Batterie 66 Ah

Kraftübertragung: Heckantrieb mit Differenzial, verblocktem Getriebe vor der Hinterachse, Kegelradantrieb (spiralverzahnt) 4-Gang-Getriebe, 2., 3. und 4. Gang synchronisiert und 1. Gang geräuscharm, Knüppelschaltung

Fahrwerk: Rechteckrohrrahmen mit Gitterrohren verstrebt, vorn Einzelradaufhängung mit Drehstabfederung und Teleskopstoßdämpfern, hinten Pendelachse mit Längsträgern, Schraubenfedern mit innenliegenden Stoßdämpfern Reifen 5,60x15 Sport

Bremsen: Fußbremse hydraulisch, auf 4 Räder wirkend, Handbremse mechanisch, auf die Hinterräder wirkend, 620 qcm Bremsfläche

Karosserie: Glasseidenverstärkte Polyester-Karosserie mit 2 Türen, Allwetterverdeck und Aufsteckscheiben für die Türen, Karosserie mit dem Fahrgestell verschweißt

Ausstattung: Kunstlederbezogene Schalensitze, Tachometer mit Tageszähler (bis 200 km/h), Drehzahlmesser, Zeituhr, Benzinuhr, Öltemperaturmesser, Zigarrenanzünder, Aschenbecher, Innen- und Außenspiegel, Kontrolleuchten, Warmluftheizung, Räder mit Kreuzspeichenblenden

Maße und Gewichte: Länge 3900 mm, Breite 1560 mm, Höhe 1150 mm, Radstand 2130 mm, Spur vorn 1305 mm, Spur hinten 1315 mm, Bodenfreiheit 170 mm, Leergewicht 580 kg, zul. Gesamtgewicht 950 kg

Geschwindigkeit: 150—160 km/h, Beschleunigung von 0 auf 100 km/h in 12 Sekunden

Verbrauch: 9 bis 11 Ltr., je nach Fahrweise

Tankinhalt: 43 Ltr.

Sonderausführung: Einbau eines Spezialkompressors und verstärkte Kurbelwelle, dadurch Leistung auf 55 DIN PS. Scheibenwaschanlage, Sperrwolf, Windschutzscheibe aus Verbundglas

Farben: Floridagelb, purpurrot, schneeweiß, rivierablau, pastellgrün

Ständige Weiterentwicklung und Verbesserungen sind ein Grundsatz der M.C.A. Automobilwerke. Deshalb sind Änderungen in Konstruktion und Ausführung gegenüber den hier gemachten Angaben vorbehalten.

Sie werden gut beraten . . . und eine Probefahrt vermittelt Ihnen:

Fotos: H. Bitterling, Eutin
Grafik und Gestaltung
Müller-Mann, Hamburg
Druck: Schneider, Plön

M.C.A. Jetstar
AUTOMOBILWERKE ULRICH OTTEN · BI
Bremen-Schönebeck   Vegesacker Heerstraße 89   Telefon 6

Colani—More Than Just a Legend

Designer Luigi Colani, still active today and as eccentric as ever, presented this extremely flat body kit for the VW Beetle. The very light synthetic body helped the 1200 version achieve quite sporting performance. The 1500, especially when tuned, could be regarded as a true sports car. However, the strange-looking car remained a borderline case, though one of the most original.

WILHELM HEUSEL Jr.
SYNTHETIC BODIES
Colani GT
a proven sports car

Colani Kit
on VW 1200 Chassis

Colani-Bausatz

auf VW-Chassis 1200

In this way capable kitmakers could build a strikingly streamlined and fast sports car on a VW chassis with comparatively little financial expenditure.

Enzmann   Schüpfheim/Lu   Schweiz

Telefon 041 86 12 22

A Beetle as a Roadster from Switzerland

Between 1957 and 1968 this Swiss variant of an open VW was on the market. Designed by Dr. Enzmann, it used the number of its stand at the Frankfurt Auto Show, 506, as its name and offered some extraordinary details.

The very individually styled roadster with a low-cost synthetic body had no side doors. One entered it via footboards on the sides. The highly arched rear also served as an upholstered headrest, and the top could be raised all the way. The Enzmann was available with a series-production 30-hp motor or, if desired, with an MAG supercharger that raised the power to 42 hp and the top speed to about 87 mph. With an optional 45-hp 1300-cc motor (tuned by the OKRASA firm) that was said to reach 100 mph, the Enzmann was perhaps too fast for the VW chassis.

Fahreigenschaften

Der mit Glasmatten verstärkte Kunstharzaufbau aus einem Stück (monobloc – mittragende Aussenhaut, stärkster Leichtbau durch Schalenbauweise der Düsenjäger) und das Ersetzen der Türe durch Trittbrettnische und Trittbügel zwischen den Sitzen, ergeben eine wesentliche Senkung des Totalgewichtes. Dadurch die rasante Beschleunigung und das Leistungsgewicht eines «Grossen». Dank Leichtbau der hochliegenden Bauteile (Plastic) kommt der Gesamtschwerpunkt tief zu liegen. Die aerodynamische Rennsportform zeichnet sich durch gute Richtungsstabilität aus, ermöglicht eine höhere Spitzengeschwindigkeit und senkt den Treibstoffverbrauch. Auch bei rascher Fahrt legt der Enzmann 506 mit dem planschfreien 55l Benzintank grosse Distanzen (750 km) ohne zu tanken zurück.

Der Enzmann 506 gibt das Gefühl von Schwerelosigkeit. Die leichtgängige Lenkung gehorcht blitzschnell, auf Passfahrten gefällt die erstaunliche Steigefähigkeit und die angenehme Bremswirkung des Motors bei starkem Gefälle.

Enzmann 506 Cabriolet

Ein 2-plätziger Sportwagen mit sicheren Fahreigenschaften, günstigem Leistungsgewicht und grossem Kofferraum – zu erschwinglichem Preise.

fast speedy economical
undemanding roomy safe

EnzmannSchüpfheim/LuzernSwitzerland

Driving characteristics

The one-piece (monobloc, load-bearing outer skin, strongest light jet-plane type of construction) synthetic resin body, strengthened with fiberglass, and the replacement of doors by footboard niches and panels between the seats result in a considerable lowering of the total weight. Thus the speedy acceleration and the performance of a "big one." Thanks to light construction of the higher body parts (plastic), the center of gravity is low. The aerodynamic racing body shows good directional stability, allows a higher top speed and decreases fuel consumption. Even when driven fast, the Enzmann 506 with the splash-free 14.5-gallon fuel tank covers great distances (466 miles) without stopping for fuel.

The Enzmann 506 gives the feeling of weightlessness. The light steering obeys instantly. When driving on mountain roads, the astonishing climbing ability and the favorable braking effect of the motor are satisfying under strong pressure.

Enzmann 506 Convertible

A 2-seat sports car with safe driving characteristics, favorable performance weight and large luggage space—at affordable prices.

Enzmann 506   Hardtop

Standard equipment

Heater and defroster
Large fast windshield wipers
Safety belts
Safety grips with map holder
Outside rear-view mirror

Advantages of doorless construction

Increased body strength and accident safety
Great decrease in weight
Easy to enter in narrow parking places
No parking damage, no crouching low to get in, no annoying noises
No drafts around knees and wrists

Advantages of the plastic body

Corrosion-free (no rust)
Sound-damping (no rattling)
Isolating (warmth, coldness)
Low repair costs (no bent metal, damage remains localized)
Great elasticity
Lighter than aluminum
Tough as steel
The basic materials are Swiss products
Synthetic resin: Oil Chemistry, Brugg
Fiberglass: Fibres de Verre S.A., Lausanne

Enzmann 506 Hardtop
    Practical, easily visible dashboard arrangement, ample room for the addition of racing instruments.
    Good access to luggage space behind the seats.
    Under the opening front hood are the fuel tank, spare wheeland tools, plus room for small luggage.

Serienausrüstung

Heizung und Defroster
Grosse, schnellgehende Scheibenwischer
Scheibenwaschanlage
Sicherheitsgurten
Sicherheitsgriffe mit Kartenhalter
Aussenrückspiegel

Vorteile der türlosen Konstruktion

Erhöhte Festigkeit und Unfallsicherheit
Grosse Gewichtssenkung
Guter Einstieg auch bei engem Parkplatz
Keine Parkschäden, kein Hineinzwängen in tiefer
Hocke, Wegfall lästiger Geräusche
Keine Zugluft auf Knie- und Handgelenke

Vorteile der Plastic-Karosserie

Korrosionsfest (kein Rosten)
Schalldämpfend (kein Dröhnen)
Isolierend (Wärme, Kälte)
Niedrige Reparaturkosten
(keine Blechverziehung, Schaden bleibt lokal)
Grosse Elastizität
Leichter als Aluminium
Zäh wie Stahl

Die Grundstoffe sind Schweizerfabrikat
Kunstharz: Oelchemie Brugg
Glasfasern: Fibres de verre S.A. Lausanne

Übersichtliche, praktische Anordnung der Armaturen, genügend Raum für den Einbau von Rennsportarmaturen.

Guter Zugang zum Kofferraum hinter den Sitzen.

Unter dem abschliessbaren Frontdeckel finden Benzintank, Reserverad und Fabrikwerkzeug nebst Kleingepäck Platz.

Vienna's Wolfgang Denzel built VW sport variations with 1300- and 1500-cc motors between 1949 and 1960, and could claim some success in international rallies. The WD 1300 convertible shown here was available from 1957 on with a 61- or 65-hp motor.

der neue denzel 1300
Serien-Super

DENZEL 1300 Super Series

The motor is a rear-mounted air-cooled 4-cylinder boxer motor which, with two Solex 40-PII double downdraft carburetors and a compression of 8.5 : 1 gives a performance of 65 hp (5400 rpm). The overhead-controlled, short-stroke motor (78 x 67 mm) produces maximum torque of 12.8 mkg at only 3800 rpm. The oil cooler is mounted in the cooling fan housing. Battery ignition. Power transmission via the dry-plate clutch to the rear-axle gearbox unified with the motor and rear axle drive, for which the most varied gear ratios are available. Exact, light shifting.

Frame is welded of profiled steel. The streamlined aluminum body has 2 or 3 seats. Independent front and rear suspension with torsion bars and telescopic shock absorbers. Hydraulic brakes with 800 cc braking surface. 15-inch wheels. Capacity of the front fuel tank 14.5 gallons. Ready-to-drive weight 1386 lbs. The power-to-weight ratio makes possible a top speed of 103 mph. Acceleration from 0 to 62 mph in 15 seconds. Fuel consumption by norm, approximately 7 quarts per 62 miles. Turning circle 31 feet.

Well-calculated dimensions give the car especially good road-holding. Wheelbase 2100 mm, front and rear track both 1310 mm, overall length 12 feet, body height (to top edge of door) 3 feet, total height (upper edge of windshield) 4 feet. Weight distribution over front and rear axles 44:56% of the car's weight.

As special equipment: slim 2-seat body, oil cooler for 9-quart circulating quantity in the nose of the car, Denzel dry-sump lubrication, special Weber 40-DCM carburetor, special brakes with 1100-cc braking surface, together with special wheels. Delivery with or without bumpers.

Winner of the International Austrian Alpine Rally 1949-1950-1952-1953-1954-1955
Winner of the International French Alpine rally 1954 and 1956

WD

Literleistung: 50 PS/ltr.
Leistungsgewicht 9,7 kg/PS

Der Motor ist ein im Heck angeordneter luftge-kühlter 4-Zylinder-Boxermotor, der mit 2 Solex-40 PII-Doppelfallstromvergasern und einer Kompression von 8,5 : 1 eine Leistung von 65 PS (5400 U/min) abgibt. Der obengesteuerte, kurz-hubig gebaute Motor (78 x 67 mm) leistet das maximale Drehmoment von 12,8 mkg bei nur 3800 U/min. Der Ölkühler ist im Gehäuse der Ge-bläsekühlung montiert. Batteriezündung. Die Kraftübertragung erfolgt über die trockene Ein-plattenkupplung zu dem mit Motor und Hinter-achsantrieb verblockten Getriebe, für das die verschiedensten Gangabstufungen lieferbar sind. Exakte, leichtgängige Mittelschaltung.

Der Rah...
windsch...
3plötzig...
abgefed...
Teleskop...
Bremsen...
15zöllige...
Tanks 5...
630 kg...
Wagen...
digkeit...
Stand e...
brauch...
durchme...

Sieger der internationalen österr...
Sieger der internationalen franz...

Denzel 1300

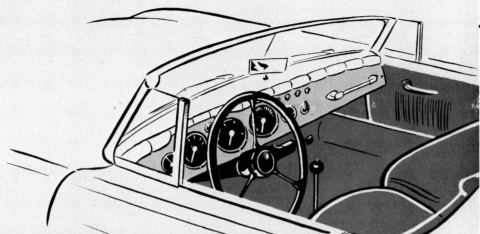

…er Wagen für den exklusiven, passio-
…ierten Fahrer. Ein einmaliges Konzept,
…n härtesten Sporteinsatz geprüft und
…eiterentwickelt. Bestes Material verarbei-
…et zu größter Präzision von Fachleuten.
…renge Kontrollen garantieren Qualität
…er Arbeit.

…roße anhaltende Motorleistung, in Ver-
…indung mit ideal ausbalanciertem
…hassis und windschlüpfiger Karosserie,
…rgibt unübertroffene Straßenlage, her-
…orragende Beschleunigung, hohe End-
…eschwindigkeit bei kleinem Verbrauch —
…deale Bedingungen für den Grand-
…ourismefahrer.

…erfeinerter Komfort und luxuriöse Aus-
…attung bieten der Dame und dem Herrn
…ptimale Bequemlichkeit im sportlichen
…eisewagen. Klare Linien, sorgfältiges
…nish, reichliche Armaturen und form-
…hönes Verdeck verleihen dem Wagen
…asse und Eleganz.

Denzel 1300
The car for the exclusive, passionate driver. A unique concept, tested and developed in the hardest sporting conditions. Best materials worked to greatest precision by experts. Strict controls guarantee quality of work.

Great lasting motor performance, along with ideally balanced chassis and streamlined body, give unbeatable roadholding, outstanding acceleration, high top speed with low consumption—ideal conditions for the grand touring driver.
Refined comfort and luxurious furnishing offer the lady and gentleman optimal comfort in a sporty touring car. Smooth lines, careful finish, ample instruments and beautiful top give the car class and elegance.
(address)

VOLFGANG DENZEL · WIEN · GRAZ · INNSBRUCK

HOF 6 · I, HEIDENSCHUSS 2 · VI, GUMPENDORFER STRASSE 19 · TEL.: U 26 2 32, U 26 2 33, U 2 20 61, A 35 0 04 · TELEGRAMMADRESSE: DENZELWERK WIEN

…K Österreichischer Werbedienst, Wien I, Strauchgasse 1 — 74041-10-56   Chwalas Druck

Super

…erschweißt. Die
…e ist 2- bis
…adaufhängung,
…mente und mit
…Hydraulische
…iche wirkend.
…ne liegenden
…engewicht ca.
…otorstärke und
…öchstgeschwin-
…ung aus dem
…m. Der Normver-
… Spurkreis-

Wohlausgewogene Abmessungen geben dem Wagen eine besonders gute Straßenlage. Radstand 2100 mm, Spurweite vorne und hinten je 1310 mm, Gesamtlänge 3650 mm, Karosseriehöhe (bis Türoberkante) 900 mm, Gesamthöhe (obere Windschutzscheibenkante) 1200 mm. Gewichtsverteilung über Vorder- und Hinterachse 44 : 56% des Wagengewichtes.
Als Sonderausstattung: Schmale 2plätzige Karosserie, Ölkühler für 8 Liter Umlaufmenge im Wagenbug, Denzel Trockensumpfschmierung, Sondervergaser Weber 40-DCM, Spezialbremsen mit 1100 cm² Belagfläche zusammen mit Spezialfelgen. Lieferung mit oder ohne Stoßstangen möglich.

Konstruktionsänderungen vorbehalten.

Alpenfahrt 1949·1950·1952·1953·1954·1955·
Alpenfahrt 1954 und 1956

rassig

racée

La voiture pour le conducteur expérimenté et passionné. Une conception unique, mise en évidence dans les plus dures épreuves sportives et développée sur cette base.
Matériel de première qualité, travail de haute précision, accompli par des spécialistes. Performances garanties par des contrôles poussés. Un haut rendement constant du moteur, secondé par un châssis parfaitement équilibré et d'une carrosserie aérodynamique, engendre une tenue de route absolument inégalable, des accélérations supérieures et une vitesse de pointe très élevée, tout en conservant une consommation minimum. Un véhicule idéal pour conducteur exigeant.

DENZEL *gewann* **die international**
DENZEL *gewann* **die international**

Although there was also a coupe version, the car of choice for customers with sporting ambitions was the bullish roadster with lowering side windows and thin top. The motor's performance was enhanced with a **Denzel** cylinderhead, and the bodywork also had been built carefully tohandle the higher stress.

racy beautiful of form
(main texts in French; at bottom, lists of rally victories, same as on previous two pages

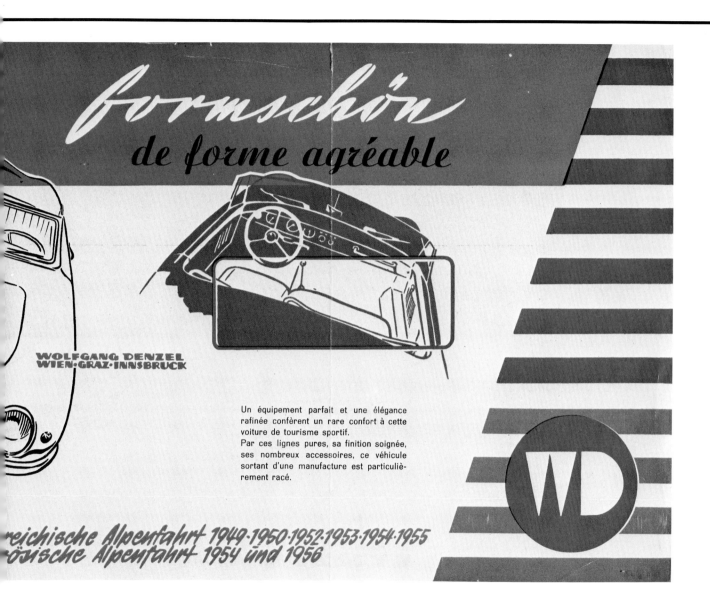

formschön

de forme agréable

WOLFGANG DENZEL
WIEN · GRAZ · INNSBRUCK

Un équipement parfait et une élégance
rafinée confèrent un rare confort à cette
voiture de tourisme sportif.
Par ces lignes pures, sa finition soignée,
ses nombreux accessoires, ce véhicule
sortant d'une manufacture est particuliè-
rement racé.

reichische Alpenfahrt 1949·1950·1952·1953·1954·1955
ösische Alpenfahrt 1954 und 1956

79

Descriptions et particularités techniques

Le moteur se trouve à l'arrière, il est du système boxer, 4 cylindres opposés à refroidissement par air. Pistons, cylindres, culasses, sont en aluminium, la pompe à essence est électrique, les carburateurs sont 2 Solex à double corps, modèle 40 P II, le graissage est assuré par circuit d'huile sous pression, refroidi par la turbine moteur. Un filtre spécial est incorporé dans ce circuit. Allumage par batterie 6 volts, 70 Ah, génératrice 130 watt.

Nombre de cyl.	4	Rendement 65 CV à 5400 t./min.	
Alésage	78 mm	Couple maximum	12,8 kgm.
Course	67 mm		à 3800 t./min.
Cylindrée	1281 cm³	Rendement au litre	50 CV
Compression	8,5 : 1	Rapport poids puissance	8,8

La transmission est assurée par un embrayage monodisque sec. La boîte, à 4 rapports, non synchronisée, forme une partie intégrale avec l'axe arrière. Démultiplication du pont arrière 4,375 : 1. Les divers rapports sont à choix. Une exécution spéciale, moyennant supplément de prix, se compose d'une carrosserie en aluminium, à 2 places, étroites, d'un système de refroidissement à huile de 8 l., d'un radiateur à l'avant, d'un système de graissage Denzel, d'une paire de double carburateurs Weber, modèle 40 DCM, d'une surface de freinage augmentée de 800 à 1100 cm2 avec tambours de freins correspondants.

Le châssis en tubes d'acier ronds et carrés, soudé, permet d'atteindre un poids minimum et une résistance maximum. Les roues avant sont fixées au châssis au moyen d'un bras oscillant. Des barres de torsion et des amortisseurs télescopiques lui confèrent une parfaite tenue de route. Les roues arrières sont fixées à l'axe oscillant, plus barres de torsion et amortisseurs télescopiques. Les freins hydrauliques agissent sur une surface de 800 cm2. Le frein à main mécanique agit sur les roues arrières. Dimension des pneus : de 500 x 15 à 640 x 15, jantes aluminium. La carrosserie est soudée au châssis. En exécution normale elle est équipée d'un siège à 3 places, fenêtres à coulisse, chauffage et capote. Sur demande, carrosserie aluminium à 2 places. Sièges agréables permettant un contact homogène avec le véhicule. Coffre d'une grande contenance derrière les sièges. Sous le capot avant, se trouve un réservoir de 55 l. et la roue de secours.

Dimensions:

Longueur	3650 mm	Hauteur	1200 mm
Voies avant		Garde au sol	180 mm
et arrières	1310 mm	Poids du véhicule	630 kg.
Empattement	2100 mm	Rayon de braquage	9,4 m
Largeur	1620 mm	Autonomie	750 km
		Vitesse max.	165 km/h.

Changement de construction réservé.

WOLFGANG DENZEL · WIEN - GRAZ - INNSBRUCK

I, AM HOF 6 · I, HEIDENSCHUSS 2 · VI, GUMPENDORFER STR. 19 · TEL.: U 26 2 32, U 26 2 33, U 22 0 61, A 35 0 04 · TELEGRAMMADR.: DENZELWERK WIEN

J. J. BUHLER
AUTOMOBILES DENZEL
LAUSANNE
Tél 228242

Chwolos Druck

1956

Österreichischer Werbedienst, Wien 1, Strauchgasse 1 — 74044-10-56

Entw. JK

This 1956 brochure printed for Switzerland in 1956 describes the most powerful 1300 type with 65 hp and top speed of almost 105 mph, called the "Super Series" and built in small numbers until 1960. A planned new coupe never went beyond prototype status.

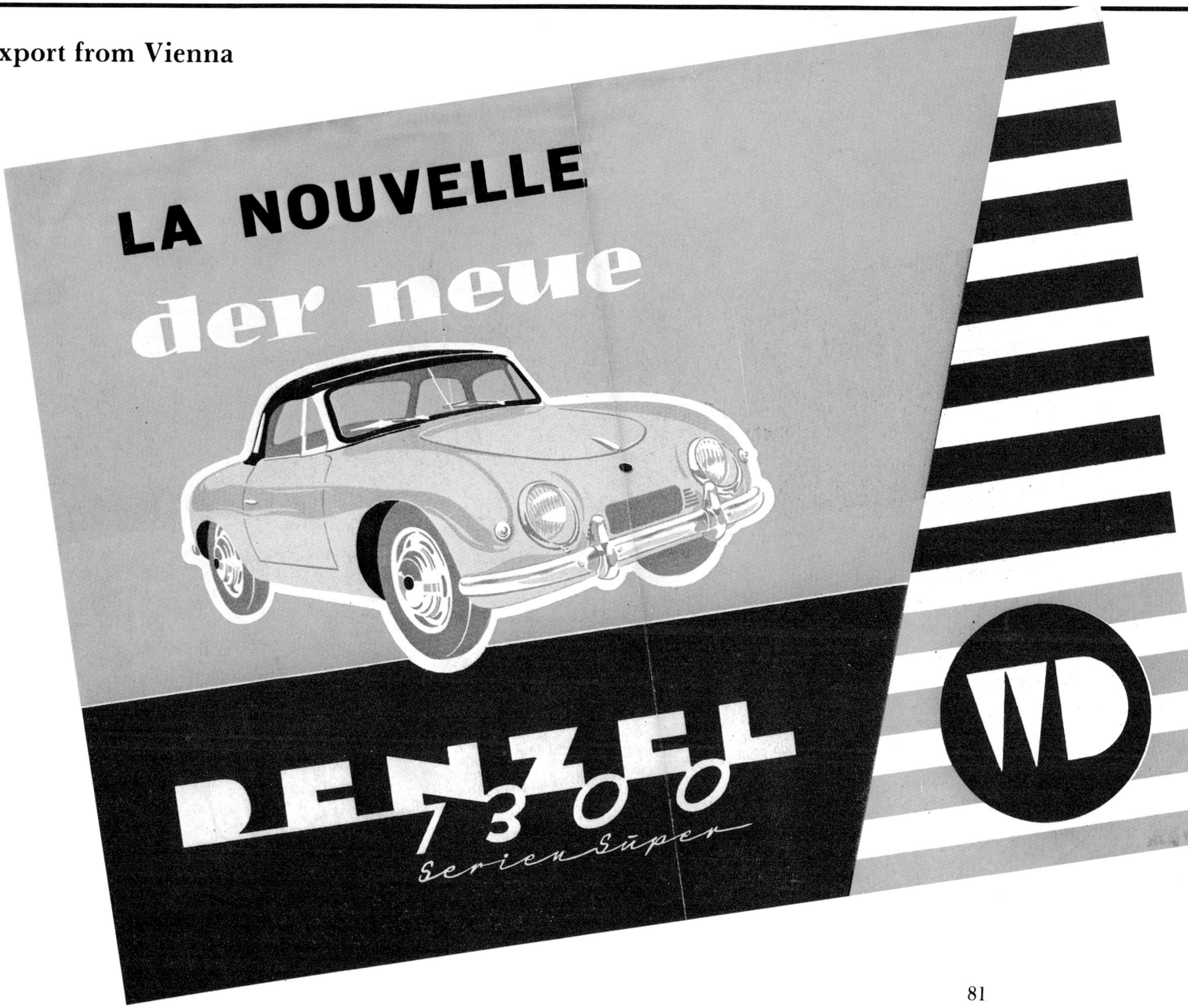

LA NOUVELLE

der neue

DENZEL 1300

Serien Super

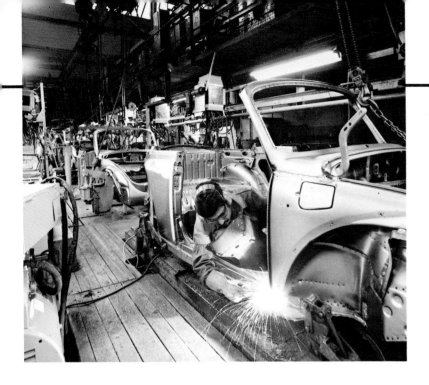

Above: Series
production of the
Beetle convertibles by
Karmann in
Osnabruck. Below: The
Karmann Ghia coupe
with vinyl top—a lot of
convertible effect on
modest means!

Right: A Hebmüller
convertible in very
good restored
condition. A desirable
collector's item.

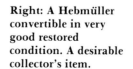

The Beetle Convertible in Miniature

The Beetle convertible was produced by many model builders, but the open Karmann Ghia remained an outsider. In Japan the open Volkswagen existed almost exclusively as a tinplate model—and scarcely was to be had in Central Europe. Among German manufacturers Wiking (plastic) and Huki (tin) particularly are noteworthy. When the Beetle convertible was modified, Wiking always kept pace in its model production. Unfortunately, the 1/40 scale Wiking Volkswagens were intended only for use by dealers, and thus not available in toy shops. The nicest models of the Karmann convertible are those of Wiking and Siku, and the same applies to the Wiking model of the Beetle convertible.

Manufacturer		Nature	Material	Scale
VW Beetle Convertible				
Bat Models	(I)	Readymade	Plastic	1/87 Hebmüller
EKO	(E)	Readymade	Plastic	1/87
Wiking	(D)	Readymade	Plastic	1/87
Jean	(D)	Readymade	Plastic	1/60
Marx	(HK)	Readymade	Metal	1/60
Tomica	(J)	Readymade	Metal	1/58 1303
Walldorf	(D)	Kit	Metal	1/45
Polistil	(I)	Readymade	Metal	1/43 1303
Rampini	(I)	Kit	Metal	1/43
Wiking	(D)	Readymade	Plastic	1/43
MC Toy	(HK)	Readymade	Metal	1/36 top down
MC Toy	(HK)	Readymade	Metal	1/36 top up
HUKI	(D)	Readymade	Tinplate	1/31 top up
A.J. Baldock	(GB)	Readymade	Bronze	1/30 1949 cvt.
A.J. Baldock	(GB)	Readymade	Bronze	1/30 Hebmüller
Diapet	(J)	Readymade	Metal	1/30 1302 S
CKO	(D)	Readymade	Tinplate	1/28
HUKI	(D)	Readymade	Tinplate	1/28
HUKI	(D)	Readymade	Tinplate	1/28 ADAC
Yodel	(J)	Kit	Plastic	1/28 Off Road
Revell	(USA)	Kit	Plastic	1/25
Bandai	(J)	Readymade	Tinplate	1/24
Imai	(J)	Kit	Plastic	1/24 1303
Polistil	(I)	Readymade	Metal	1/24 1303
Shinsei	(J)	Readymade	Tinplate	1/20 ca. 1963
TN	(Toy Namura, J)	Readymade	Tinplate	1/20 ca. 1963
Taiyo	(J)	Readymade	Tinplate	1/18 1954
TN	(Toy Namura, J)	Readymade	Tinplate	1/16 ca. 1954
Bandai	(J)	Readymade	Tinplate	1/15 1954
Dinky	(D)	Readymade	Plastic	1/15 ca. 1954
Karmann Ghia Convertible				
Wiking	(D)	Readymade	Plastic	1/87
Siku	(D)	Readymade	Plastic	1/60
Wiking	(D)	Readymade	Plastic	1/40
Yonezawa Diapet	(J)	Readymade	Metal	1/40
Bandai	(J)	Readymade	Tinplate	1/20

The Beetle as Seen in the Press

In general, paeans of praise, sometimes pages long, have been written and published for fifty years about riding in open cars. But then it gradually became old-fashioned to drive open cars. In the seventies there were only a few manufacturers who still included a convertible in their programs. But three prominent producers always have included an open car in their catalogs: Alfa Romeo, Mercedes-Benz and Volkswagen.

The Volkswagen firm always was modest in its publicity work during the fifties. The lively advertising texts and grandiose international campaigns began much later. At the end of 1952, Werner Oswald wrote in the magazine *Auto, Motor and Sport*: "From whatever considerations the Volkswagen firm always has conducted its limited advertising, today this fact is really a relief to us. When we commence today to write up an unusually positive test of the VW, then at least nobody can say of us that 'you fellows do it only because of the advertising.' As little as we otherwise feel the effect of such accusations, in this case we have the advantage of not even having appearances speak against us."

"Of what car could one say that it still not only is

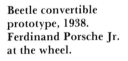

Beetle convertible
prototype, 1938.
Ferdinand Porsche Jr.
at the wheel.

built almost unchanged fifteen years after it first appeared, but also still enjoys growing popularity?'' the author wrote. "We often have told how much we treasure the VW, as in our last test report of 1951. Since last October the Volkswagen has been improved significantly again in many aspects. Above all, the Volkswagen firm now has answered its customers' most frequent wish and equipped the car with a synchronized transmission. Among other noticeable changes the new dashboard, the vent windows, a new carburetor with accelerator pump, fifteen-inch wheel rims with low-pressure tires, and new bumpers can be mentioned. Many other detail changes were put into production at the same time.''

About the qualities—and also the disadvantages—of the Beetle, the testers are always in agreement with the everyday users. In the fall of 1955 *Auto, Motor and Sport* said: "Once again driving a Volkswagen for three weeks gave the tester a definite pleasure, no matter if he has to do mostly with larger and, though less familiar, also more interesting cars.'' Just the certainty that one does not have to expect any particular surprises—"in either a positive or a negative sense''—had a reassuring effect. The motor journalist referred particularly to the subject of a side-view mirror.

"Since the Volkswagen factory often has served as a good example, especially in questions of equipment and accessories, of being ready to make additional developments, and not merely when under pressure,

Left: Hessian ADAC Winter Rally, 1956. Harald von Saucken taking part in a 1955 convertible.

we would have welcomed it most gratefully if the new VW had finally been put into series production with an outside mirror. One automobile factory must eventually make the start, and the Volkswagen factory is, after all, the biggest in Germany. The outside mirror is a necessary accessory for traffic safety on all cars without exception, but most necessary of all on the VW, which lacks glass all around. We drove the test car, which a dealer handed over to us at the request of the factory, only after a mirror was quickly attached to it.''

In fact, though, this outside mirror was the only accessory that one missed on the Volkswagen. Otherwise nothing was missing, and it is precisely in terms of equipment that it showed itself to be clearly superior to all its competitors at home and abroad. One may understand fully that a car like the VW must be limited to what is necessary, but that is what is there. ''Or would someone assert that the one instrument present, a speedometer, was not enough? One can easily do without a clock; a thermometer is not necessary for an air-cooled motor; the good old three-way valve is also a bit much for us today, to say nothing of the gas gauges that, as experience shows, are never completely reliable. But the Volkswagen does have front and rear ashtrays, a sun visor for the driver, strong handholds on the doors, and proper coat hooks left and right. Of course the last, for example, are a mere bagatelle, but why does one look for them in vain in other cars?''

Right: Three-quarter rear view of the Hebmüller two-seater shown on page 83.

Above: The Beetle convertible collection of a fan club. The exception is the very old sedan at the extreme left.

The Volkswagen may have been praised or criticized—but it was a phenomenon, and the leading men in Wolfsburg were numbered among the "makers" of the German Economic Miracle. The chief of the firm was Heinz Nordhoff, about whom *der Spiegel* wrote: "He is a vicious circle on whom the Wolfsburgers roll into the future. Because the Volkswagen is a success, no competition exists—because no competition exists, the model does not need to be changed—because it stays the same, its resale value is very high—and because this value is so high, the model remains the same. Dr. Nordhoff was made an honorary citizen of the City of Wolfsburg in 1955 on the occasion of the production of the millionth Volkswagen. He also was awarded the Grand Cross of the Federal Achievement Cross with a star.

Nordhoff once said that the millionth Volkswagen would not look different from the five-hundred-thousandth. Naturally, he kept his word. At that time there even were price reductions. The daily press rejoiced: "The export sedan has become 250 Marks cheaper, the standard sedan 160!" The convertible became 510 Marks cheaper. As of August 1955 it cost only 5990 Marks.

The price reduction stood in opposition to the constantly increasing costs of salaries and materials, the VW publicity department announced. The large series production of 1280 cars per day in 1955 nevertheless allowed a favorable calculation: "In a year and a half we'll build 1500 cars a day!"

Right: Racy roadsters were built again and again by individual initiative, like this polyester-bodied example.

In 1953 and again in 1955 the testers stressed the fact that there really were no more possible wishes for the Volkswagen. Even if its body style was regarded as old-fashioned: "It may well be the last car to have real fenders and a flat windshield." At the end of 1957 one was more critical: "Today the space and sight conditions of cars of this size are usually different.... The street- and road holding of the VW is no longer likely to be accepted without reservations...." One spoke of the "usual deficiencies of the trade" that one was consciously ready to overlook because driving the car was a lot of fun! The characteristic weaknesses of the VW were balanced by equally characteristic advantages "such as are offered by no other comparable car." Less than two-and-a-half gallons of fuel consumption on average per 62 miles ("higher than in previous years") still was regarded as in order, just as the cost of maintenance in general had such a good relationship to the performance that one would be a fool to deny it. As people had said for a

Photo motif number one: pretty girls on board an open car. Convertible drivers always have a full load....

long time. This led to interesting resale prices. The Beetle could not be killed, in the end, because of the Wolfsburg motto: "It runs and runs and runs...."

In a comparison of convertibles on the market, the *Cologne Auto Journal* said in May 1974: "Regrettably, the choice decreases from year to year because safety apostles in the USA, and recently in Europe too, spoil the pleasure of new creation for constructors and builders of fresh-air cars." Werner Müller said of the VW convertible: "With four seats, very good workmanship and a better-than-average resale value, the Beetle convertible is predestined for a family with a thirst for fresh air." Unfortunately the car now cost over 10,000 Marks. In comparison the open Fiat X 1/9 cost 11,590 Marks, the convertible based on the Peugeot 304 cost 9950 Marks. In all countries of the Western world the Beetle was the subject of exhaustive test reports. *Modern Motors* (Melbourne, Australia) wrote in 1973: "The Volkswagen has a few strong plus points to show: best workmanship, first-class finish. It is reliable, simple to maintain and also very economical. With its looks, it will not go out of style soon."

Foreign reporters became downright euphoric about the Karmann Ghia. The car obviously was particularly well received in the English-speaking countries. *Motor Trend* called the 1967 model "the little man's Porsche." Incidentally, this model was tuned to 105 horsepower, which turned the Osnabrück two-seater into a 103-mph speedster at a cost of 600 dollars.

Classic and Sports Car said in the summer of 1982: "The Karmann Ghia is the embodiment of a beautiful butterfly that emerges from an ugly Beetle. Not a rare car—too many of them have been built—but a picture-pretty and in every way collectable one. The older models still have a high value to fans today." This corresponds completely to the facts.

The sedan-based convertible built by Eller of Ober-Ramstadt.

Phases of Development of the VW Beetle Convertible 1949-1980

1949	Production starts on June 3, 1131-cc 25-hp motor; as of October delivered without a starting crank, with roller-type gas pedal.
1950	As of January thickening between headlights and fenders; as of April oleo-pressure brakes (previously cable); as of June an ashtray over the starter button.
1951	As of April vent openings behind the front fenders, Wolfsburg arms on the front hood, telescopic instead of strut shock absorbers, stronger generator; as of November no more armrests for the rear seats.
1952	As of October 2nd, 3rd and 4th gears synchronized; front vent windows; new dashboard design; glove compartment with door and push button; brake lights now at the top of the taillight housings; bigger windshield wipers; turn signal lever and starter button now to the left of the steering wheel.
1953	As of January oil-bath air filter; as of March an ashtray with a small handle integral with the dashboard; as of December an 1192-cc 30-hp motor, automatic and controllable instrument lighting, combined ignition and starter lock.
1954	As of May resin instead of nitro finish, two sun visors, top boot without fold in seat, new seat upholstery.
1955	As of August muffler with two tailpipes, new easier-to-grip steering wheel with deep spokes, bent gearshift lever, wider front seats, seat backs adjustable to three positions, new leatherette interior upholstery with borders, rear lights mounted 6 cm higher. Karmann Ghia coupe production begins in August.
1956	As of July tubeless tires; as of September top fastening pins of brass instead of iron; as of October standard side-view mirror.
1957	As of September steering wheel with horn ring, turn signal turns off automatically combined with flasher; as of August gas pedal instead of roller, vent louvers horizontal instead of vertical, windshield bigger by about 8 percent, rear window by about 45 percent, longer wiper blades. Karmann Ghia convertible production begins August 1.
1958	As of January ivory disc wheels; as of February US version with front and rear bumper protectors. Karmann Ghia convertible with dashboard padded at top, fuel gauge, new steering wheel with horn ring.
1959	As of August steering wheel with two spokes and deep hub, door handles with locking knobs, removable rear wall with window, 180- instead of 160-watt generator.

1960	As of March cords in hollows of top seams, top frame as far as main frame; as of August 34-hp motor, new screw-on top catches, speedometer to 87 mph (formerly 75), windshield wiper-washer system; as of November front directional light amber instead of white. Karmann Ghia convertible with 34-hp motor, fully synchronized gears.
1961	As of May combined tail-brake-directional lights in two-section design; as of July gas gauge; as of November conical gearshift with small knob.
1962	As of April improved hydraulic brake system; as of July bigger fuel line in cylinder head.
1963	As of August horn button instead of ring, VW hubcap emblem no longer painted, seats with synthetic instead of wool upholstery; as of October bigger directional lights on the front fenders.
1964	Slight enlargement of the window surfaces.
1965	Improved front axle, defroster vent in the center of the dashboard, pierced wheels. Karmann Ghia convertible has 1.3-liter 40-hp motor, modified front axle.
1966	Shorter motor hood without raised center, new door handles, one-key system. Karmann Ghia convertible has 1.5-liter 44-hp motor, front disc brakes, dual-circuit braking system.
1967	Vertical headlights, new bumpers, fuel filler cap on the right front sidewall, new door locks with inside knobs, dashboard padding, dual-circuit braking system, shorter shift lever, safety steering column.
1968	Interior hood release, opening rear window of safety glass, top catches at sides of top frame.
1969	Additional fresh air vents on the hood (28). Karmann Ghia convertible has square front directional lights.
1970	Larger trunk space; additional fresh air vents on dashboard; spring front suspension; 1.6-liter 50-hp motor, also for Karmann Ghia convertible.
1971	Slightly changed engine hood, now with 26 louvers; safety steering wheel with four spokes; new windshield wiper-washer lever on right side of steering column. Karmann Ghia convertible has new box-section bumpers.
1972	Completely new dashboard, strongly arched windshield, big round taillights.
1973	Beetle convertible only available as Type 1303 LS.
1974	Front directional lights set in bumper, convertible only available as Type 1303, black exhaust pipes. Karmann Ghia convertible production ends in March.
1975-1979	No major changes except in color choices.
1980	Beetle convertible production ends January 10.

Volckswagen Beetle Clubs

Interessengemeinschaft der Karmann-Ghia-Fahrer
Uwe Witkowski, Im Schmidtenstück 14,
5401 Ney, West Germany

Klub der Käfer-Freunde e. V.
Michael Mösslang, Postweg 38,
8000 München 82, West Germany

VW Uralt-Käfer-Club Schweiz
J. Eberhard, Tennenstrasse 14,
CH-9032 Engelberg, Switzerland

VW Split Window Club U.K.
Jim Murray, 29 Idmiston Sq.,
Worcester Park, Surrey KT4 7SX, England

Club International des Cabriolets Volkswagen
C.C.V.W/, 8, rue de la Mérantaise
F-78960 Voisins-le-Bretonneux, France

Vintage VW Registry 1938-55
Steve H. Wood, P.O. Box 16 308
Seattle, Washington 98116 USA

Brezelfenster-Vereinigung e.V.
E. P. Hagen, Amselweg 4, 3073 Liebenau, West
Germany

Bonner Käfer-Cabrio-Club e.V.
J. Vogel, Bonner Talweg 28, 5300 Bonn 1, West
Germany

VW Käfer Cabrio-Club
F. Otte, Weitkampweg 81, 4500 Osnabrück, West
Germany

Karmann Ghia Club Austria
R. Gravogel, Hippgasse 25/19, A-1160 Vienna,
Austria

VW Veteranenklub Danmark
Mosevagn 105, DK-5330 Munkebo, Denmark

VW Club Nederland
Bussumsestraat 96, NL-2575 JM 's Gravenhage,
Netherlands

Volkswagenhistoriska Klubben
Rohallsvagen 34, S-18363 Taby, Sweden

Vintage Volkswagen-Club of America
817 5th Street, Cresson PA 16630 USA

VW Convertible Bibliography

Der Käfer I—Eine Dokumentation—Die Modelle von 1945 bis 1982 by H.-R. Etzold. This first volume includes all technical data and details in their yearly changes in production. Over 80,000 detail changes were carried out in the course of Beetle production. 224 pages, 250 illustrations.

Der Käfer II—Eine Dokumentation. Die Käfer-Entwicklung von 1934 to 1982 by H.-R. Etzold. The development of the original model to today's world champion completes the first typological volume. 200 pages, many illustrations.

Der Käfer III—Eine Dokumentation. This volume reports on the fastest, longest, widest and most original Beetles. 220 pages, 230 photos.

Das Grosse Buch der Volkswagen-Typen: Alle Fahrzeuge von 1934 bis heute by Lothar Boschen. This is the complete history of the Volkswagen to 1983. All prototypes and series models are treated, with their variants. 588 pages, approx. 600 photos.

Volkswagen-Käfer—das 20-Millionending aus Wolfsburg. An authentic documentation by authors Borgeson, Shuler and Sloniger. For the first time the complete background story of the Beetle's origin. Examples of technology, advertising, and history. German edition of a publication highly praised in the USA (Automobile Quarterly). 168 pages, 48 in color.

Die VW-Story by Jerry Sloniger. Everything about the development of the Beetle in historical and technical aspects. The models are traced from the first prototype to the VW Golf and described in detail. 288 pages, 175 illustrations.

Volkswagen Bug! The People's Car by Ray Miller. From the renowned Evergreen Series, with many useful and informative detail photos that can help you identify your model. All models portrayed—from the prewar Beetle to 1979. 320 pages, 1400 illustrations.

Eine Woche im Volkswagenwerk—80 Fotografien aus dem April 1953 by Peter Keetman. Edited by Rolf Sachsse. Approx. 96 pages, 80 black-and-white photos.

VW Beetle and Karmann Ghia: A Collector's Guide by Jonathan Wood. Like every volume a wealth of information about the model's development. Tips for buying, restoring and maintaining value. 128 pages, 150 illustrations.

Is The Bug Dead? The Great Beetle Ad Campaign. An exciting collection of advertisements from America that deal mainly with Beetle motifs but also with the Karmann Ghia, the bus and the 411. 144 pages, 125 illustrations.

Volkswagen Pocket History by Stefan Woltereck. In this small but superbly compiled one-brand volume, the entire developmental history of the Volkswagen to 1982 is presented. 72 pages, 80 black-and-white and 8 color photos.

Volkswagen Cars by R. M. Clarke. Several volumes on Volkswagens have appeared in the Brooklands Series. Every volume consists of reprints of contemporary road tests and publications and offers a wealth of technical and historical documents. Every volume has 100 pages, with many illustrations.

Volkswagen Cars 1936-56.   Same as above.

VW Beetle 1956-77.   Same as above.

VW Karmann Ghia 1956-73.   Same as above.

VW Karmann Ghia 1955-82.   Same as above.

Dein KDF-Wagen. Reprint of the 1939 sales brochure. 32 pages, 48 black-and-white photos and 6 drawings.

Der Käfer by Arthur Railton. An unusual auto and its unusual success. A Eurotax Book. 222 pages, 30 illustrations.

Das Grosse Käfer-Buch—A paperback book by Peter Lanz. The Volkswagen story in compact form. 174 pages.

Allerwelts-Wagen—The history of the automotive economic miracle by Ulrich Kubisch. A richly illustrated book filled with many facts and much data. 128 pages, softcover.

VW Käfer 1951 (24 PS). Reprint of the manual for the "Pretzel-window Beetle," sedan and convertible.

VW Käfer 1954 (30 PS). Reprint of the manual for sedan and convertible.

VW Käfer 1966-1983—Technik, Wartung, Reparatur by Hans-Jürgen Schneider. This repair handbook appeared in pocket form in the BLV Auto and Motorcycle Series. 127 pages, 215 photos in black-and-white and color.

Volkswagen Käfer (1200/1300/1302/1302S/1303/1303S/1500/ 1600/Karmann Ghia 181) 68-74. Bucheli Repair Manual no. 198/199.

VW Käfer (1200/1300/1500) bis 7/69. Now I help myself, Korp Volume 1.

VW Käfer 1200-1303S ab 8/69. Now I help myself, Korp Volume 26.

VW Käfer 1200/1300/1500/1302/1302S/1303/1303S. Now I do it faster, Korp Volume 7.

VW Käfer (Alle Modelle). How to do it. Etzold Volume 16.

VW Käfer: V.A.G. Handbook. In cooperation with the ADAC Publishing House, a useful do-it-yourself manual for the care and repair of all Beetle models. 248 pages, 262 illustrations, 2 plans.

Volkswagen 1939-1967 (1100/1200/1300/Karmann Ghia). Repair manual in the Collector's Archives Series, French.

VW Karmann Ghia Modell 1960. Assembly manual only for body construction; all differences in the Beetle are treated. 150 pages, reprint.

VW Karmann Ghia 1500/44 PS Coupé und Cabrio 1968. Reprint of the factory manual.

VW Karmann Ghia 1200/30 PS Limousine und Cabrio 1950. Reprint of the factory manual.

VW Karmann Ghia 1200 Baujahr 1963. Reprint of the factory manual. 76 pages.

DEUTSCHMARK/DOLLAR CONVERSION CHART

YEAR	DEUTSCHMARKS PER DOLLAR
1954	4.1946
1956	4.2034
1958	4.1876
1960	4.2
1962	4.0
1964	3.9745
1966	4.0
1968	4.0
1970	3.6600
1972	3.2225
1974	2.5100
1976	2.5906
1978	2.0820
1980	1.7793
1982	2.3702
1984	2.7300
1986	2.3218
1988	1.7316
1989	1.8625

All figures note number of Deutschmarks equivalent to U.S. dollar at then-current exchange rates.